Athenian Democracy

IN THE SAME SERIES

General Editors: Eric J. Evans and P.D. King

LANCASTER PAMPHLETS

Athenian Democracy

John Thorley

London and New York

First published 1996
by Routledge
11 New Fetter Lane, London EC4P 4EE

Simultaneously published in the USA and Canada
by Routledge
29 West 35th Street, New York, NY 10001

© *1996 John Thorley*

Typeset in Bembo by
Ponting–Green Publishing Services, Chesham, Bucks
Printed and bound in Great Britain by
Clays Ltd, St. Ives PLC

British Library Cataloguing in Publication Data
A catalogue record for this book is available from
the British Library

Library of Congress Cataloguing in Publication Data
Thorley, John, 1940–
Athenian Democracy / John Thorley.
p. cm.- (Lancaster pamphlets)
Includes bibliographical references.
1. Democracy–Greece–Athens–History.
2. Athens (Greece)–Politics and government.
I. Title. II. Series.
JC75.D36T56   1996
320.438'5–dc20   96–3287

ISBN 0–415–12967–2

Contents

vii

Foreword

Lancaster Pamphlets offer concise and up-to-date accounts of major historical topics, primarily for the help of students preparing for Advanced Level examinations, though they should also be of value to those pursuing introductory courses in universities and other institutions of higher education. Without being all-embracing, their aims are to bring some of the central themes or problems confronting students and teachers into sharper focus than the textbook writer can hope to do; to provide the reader with some of the results of recent research which the textbook may not embody; and to stimulate thought about the whole interpretation of the topic under discussion.

Preface

This book is designed for those who want to know how the Athenian democracy was devised and in particular how it operated during the fifth century BC. Most students of Greek history concentrate their attention on the fifth century, with the Persian Wars, the Athenian Empire, the Peloponnesian War and the great dramatists and historians as the main topics for study. But for the study of Athenian democracy the concentration on this period does present some problems, since we do in fact have more information about the workings of the democracy from the latter half of the fourth century BC, mainly because of numerous inscriptions from that period and also because we possess so many of Demosthenes' political speeches, from his first speech in 352 until his death in 322. Many general descriptions of Athenian democracy therefore tend to concentrate on how it operated in the time of Demosthenes, and in some respects this was rather different from what happened in the fifth century. This book, however, assumes that most students will want to know how the democracy worked in the period they are most likely to study, and whilst it does not aim to be an exhaustive study of Athenian democracy, it presents a chronologically based account of the development of Athenian government up to the end of the Peloponnesian War, linking this development with the main events and prominent people of the time, and it is based as far as possible on evidence which refers to the situation up to 404. The history, the society and the culture of Athens in the classical period cannot be properly understood without reference to the contemporaneous development of its democratic system of government, and it is hoped that this book will contribute to that understanding.

Notes

1 The transcription of Greek words and names is always a problem. In many cases Greek orthography has been followed, but well established English forms (e.g. Athens, Pericles) have been retained.

2 Where Greek words (other than names) are used, these are printed in *italics*, and the meaning is explained in the text.

3 All translations from Greek writers are by the author.

Date chart

The following date chart shows on the right the sequence of the main Athenian democratic reforms discussed in the text, and on the left some of the key events in the history of Athens during the same period.

Key events	Athenian democratic reforms
*c.*632: Kylon's conspiracy	
*c.*621: Codification of laws by Drakon	
594: Solon's arkhonship	594 (or a few years later): Solon's reforms
560–527: Peisistratos tyrant	
527: Hippias becomes tyrant	
514: Assassination of Hipparkhos, Hippias' brother	
510: Expulsion of Hippias	
508: Isagoras appointed arkhon, but expelled by Alkmeonids	508/7: Reforms of Kleisthenes
499: Revolt of Ionian Greeks against Persian rule, followed by Persian Wars	
490: Battle of Marathon	
	487/6: Arkhons to be chosen by lot

Key events	Athenian democratic reforms
483: Themistocles persuades Assembly to use silver from Laureion to develop fleet	
480: Battles of Thermopylae and Salamis	
479: Battles of Plataea and Mykale; establishment of Delian League	
	462/1: Ephialtes' reforms of the Council of the Areopagos
461: Ostracism of Kimon; Assassination of Ephialtes; rise of Pericles	
454: Treasury of Delian League moved from Delos to Athens	
	453/2(?): Reintroduction of 'deme-judges'
	451/50: Introduction of pay for dikasts (probably also for members of the *Boule* and other magistrates). Pericles' law restricting citizenship to those whose parents were both Athenian
449: Peace with Persia (Peace of Kallias)	
431: Outbreak of Peloponnesian War	
429: Death of Pericles	
	420s: Likely date of 'The Old Oligarch'
411/10: Oligarchy in Athens	411/10: Democracy suspended during Oligarchy
	410: Codification of law begun (completed 399)
404: Peloponnesian War ends in defeat of Athens; 'Thirty Tyrants' take over government of Athens	404/3: Democracy suspended during rule of 'Thirty Tyrants'.
	403/2: Introduction of payment for attendance at meetings of the Assembly
	399: Board of *nomothetai* introduced to deal with new legislation

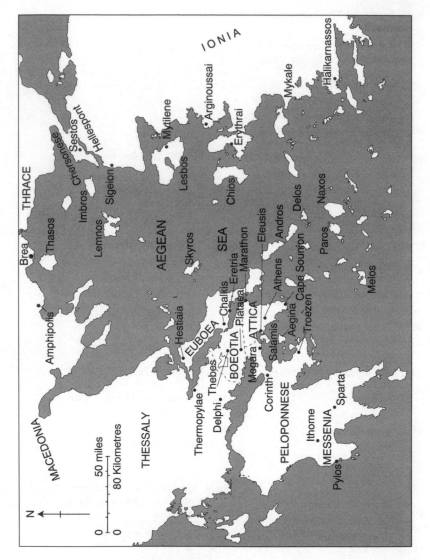

Map 1 Greece, the Aegean and Ionia

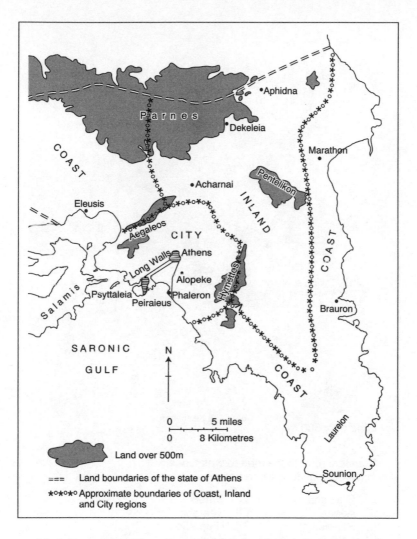

Map 2 ATTICA: City, Coast and Inland regions as defined
by Kleisthenes' reforms of 508/7 BC

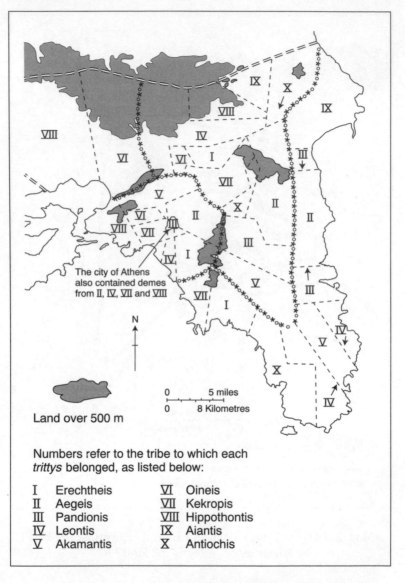

The city of Athens
also contained demes
from II, IV, VII and VIII

N

0   5 miles
0   8 Kilometres

Land over 500 m

Numbers refer to the tribe to which each
trittys belonged, as listed below:

I	Erechtheis	VI	Oineis
II	Aegeis	VII	Kekropis
III	Pandionis	VIII	Hippothontis
IV	Leontis	IX	Aiantis
V	Akamantis	X	Antiochis

Map 3 ATTICA: City, Coastal and Inland *trittyes*

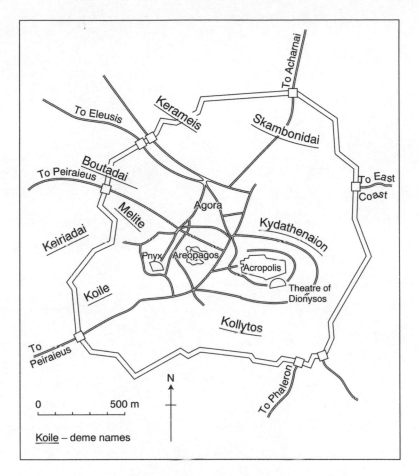

Map 4 The city of Athens

1
Introduction

In the fifth century BC Athens and the rest of Attica had a total
population of probably around 250,000–300,000. Attica measured about fifty miles from the border with Boeotia in the north-
west to Cape Sounion in the south-east, and about thirty miles
from Eleusis in the south-west to the northern tip of the Bay of
Marathon on the north-east coast (see Map 1). This is roughly
the same population and geographical size as, in England,
Carlisle and the northern half of Cumbria, or Norwich and the
eastern half of Norfolk, or, in the United States, about half the
size of the state of Delaware. What is remarkable about the
small state of Athens and Attica is that 2,500 years ago its
inhabitants created, for a period of about two hundred years, a
society of such vision and achievements that they have ever
since been the subjects of detailed study and, almost universally,
of admiration. What did the Athenians do to deserve such
attention?

Until the fifth century the achievements of the people of
Athens and Attica were in fact not particularly distinguished.
Athens and Attica had been united into one city-state probably
during the course of the eighth century BC. The local tradition
was that the unification had been achieved by the legendary king
Theseus well before the Trojan War (which would put it around
1300 BC during the Mycenaean period), but if this does reflect
a historical reality it is nevertheless likely that the unification

1

had to be re-done after the chaos which followed the collapse of the Mycenaean kingdoms. The eighth century is no more than a reasonable guess; it may have been earlier, though hardly later. But then from the eighth to the middle of the sixth century, when many other city-states were busily establishing colonies around the shores of the Mediterranean and into the Black Sea, Athens was strangely uninvolved. Perhaps the citizens of Athens and Attica did not feel they needed to spread overseas; perhaps they were just not organised enough to do it. Again, in the field of literature the seventh and sixth centuries saw the flowering of lyric poetry (poems by a solo performer accompanied by a lyre or other instrument) in most parts of the Greek-speaking world. We have substantial fragments from about twenty poets, from Ionia, from the Aegean islands, from Sparta and Megara, and from South Italy. But from Athens we have only Solon (the great constitutional reformer) and, if one is prepared to go down to 500 BC, a shadowy figure called Apollodoros who is now represented by just a line and a half. Of the known philosophers of the sixth century (and we have substantial information about Thales, Anaximander, Anaximenes, Xenophanes, Herakleitos and Pythagoras, all of them from the Ionian coast of Asia Minor) not one apparently even visited Athens. We certainly do not get the impression that Athens (and by that we now mean Athens and Attica) is the centre of Greek culture in the eighth, seventh, or sixth centuries. But the fifth century is something quite different, and we must seek explanations.

Any explanations of a complex phenomenon such as fifth-century Athenian culture will themselves be complex, but underlying the phenomenon is the political system which the Athenians shaped for themselves, their democracy. It would be far too simplistic to suggest that the democracy was the sole reason for the flowering of Athenian culture, if only because other states later developed democracies but did not suddenly flourish culturally. But Athenian democracy was the first democracy; it was in many ways a radical democracy, and it was seen by many, probably most, Athenians as an integral part of their cultural achievements, as Pericles' famous funeral oration in the autumn of 431 testifies (Thucydides 2.35–46).

The democracy was brought into being by Kleisthenes in 508/7 after thirty-six years of one-man rule in Athens by the

2

tyrants Peisistratos, who was much respected for his abilities, and his son Hippias, who was hardly respected at all. The political background to Kleisthenes' reforms and his likely motives will be analysed later; for the moment we may simply note that the changes were indeed revolutionary and gave all male citizens of Athens quite unprecedented powers – in fact absolute powers in a corporate sense – over policy, finance and the whole legal system, which is to say over the whole running of the state of Athens; and we may also note that Kleisthenes probably did not quite intend it that way! But the sudden change from one-man rule could hardly have been greater, and the Athenians took to their new system with great enthusiasm.

Only a few years later the Athenians were embroiled with the massive power of the recently founded Persian Empire, and the Persian Wars which followed moulded the minds of Athenians, inspiring them with self-confidence (which often appeared to others as arrogance) and offering opportunities for political power which they took with enthusiasm. In 498 Athens had helped the Ionian Greeks in their revolt against their new Persian masters, thus incurring the enmity of the Persian king, Darius, who sent a force to attack Attica. It landed at Marathon in 490 and was heroically defeated; 6,400 Persians were killed, with the loss of only 192 Athenians. Ten years later Darius' son Xerxes sent a much larger force: an army of disputed size but undoubtedly very large by any standards and a fleet of over 1,200 ships, which attacked Greece along the coast of the north Aegean then into Thessaly and on to Central Greece. The Persians occupied Athens and totally destroyed the city after most of the population had been evacuated to the island of Salamis and to the friendly town of Troezen on the southern shores of the Saronic Gulf. The Spartan king Leonidas (one of the two kings of Sparta; they had a quaint system of two royal families) with his small force of Spartans had gained great glory by delaying the Persian advance at Thermopylae in Central Greece. But the decisive battle was the naval battle fought in the narrow waters round Salamis in the late summer of 480, where the mainly Athenian fleet defeated the superior numbers of the Persian fleet through the clever strategy of the Athenian Themistocles. The Persian land forces were still intact, though now in a difficult position, and were defeated at Plataea in Central Greece the following spring.

3

The importance of the Persian Wars for the development of Athenian culture is worth stressing. The Athenians remembered Marathon and Salamis as their finest hours; and the fact that one was a land battle and the other a sea battle was also of great significance, because while Marathon had been won by the hoplites, who came from the wealthier classes, Salamis had been won by the rowers of the triremes, who came from the poorer classes. Athenians saw the defeat of the Persians as a triumph for their democratic system of government.

And there was a further point – or rather two linked points. The Persians had destroyed the city of Athens, its houses, temples, public buildings and city walls, but the Athenian fleet of trireme warships was still largely intact. During the following years Athens established the Delian League consisting of most of the Aegean islands and seaboard towns of the Aegean as a defence against possible future Persian aggression, with its fleet as the great deterrent. But when Athens formally made peace with Persia in 449 and all pretence of a defence league was gone, the citizens of the democracy nevertheless had no qualms (or very few) about putting the annual revenues from their allies into rebuilding the temples of the city on a magnificent scale.

Art and architecture and drama and literature and philosophy flourished. And they continued to flourish throughout the Peloponnesian War which resulted from the increasing tension between Athens and the Peloponnesian League, a war which Pericles saw as inevitable. But he died only two years after the war began, and no such dominant leader was found to replace him. Athenian blunders, combined with increasing naval competence on the part of Sparta, led to the humiliating defeat of Athens in 404. Though a democratic system of government did continue in Athens, its empire was gone and so was its confidence.

Kleisthenes' democratic system gave Athenian citizens quite unprecedented freedom to express their opinions and to make their own decisions. They were just learning to do this when the Persian Wars came along and not only left them with memories of heroic splendour but forced political opportunities upon them and convinced them of the superiority of their democratic system. It was against this background that the Athenians built their empire, developed their unique expression of civilisation and fought their wars. If we are to understand the history and cultural achievements of fifth-century Athens we must see how their democracy actually worked.

2

Prelude to democracy

Athens before Solon

Thucydides, the great historian of the Peloponnesian War, asserts without question that it was Theseus, a king of Athens in the period before the Trojan War, who unified Athens and Attica into one *polis*. The process was traditionally referred to as *sunoikismos*, 'living together', and Thucydides describes it in some detail (Thucydides 2.14.1–2.15.2 and 2.16.1). Many modern historians have questioned Thucydides' version of the *sunoikismos*, arguing that even if there was a Mycenaean unification of Attica it probably needed to be done again after the collapse of the Mycenaean world. There certainly seems to be evidence that Eleusis in the west and Marathon on the east coast were incorporated into Attica after the Mycenaean period, but this does not necessarily mean that Attica had been entirely fragmented and had to be reconstituted as a unified state. The truth may be that most of Attica did remain united after the Mycenaean period, but that some extremities had to be re-incorporated, perhaps during the eighth century; if it had been later than that one would have expected some clearer historical tradition of which Thucydides would surely have been aware.

In describing the process of *sunoikismos* Thucydides makes a point which we should always bear in mind about the population of Attica:

So for a long time the Athenians had lived in independent communities throughout Attica, and even after their unification the common experience from the time of the ancient inhabitants right down to the present war was to be born and to live in the country.

(Thucydides 2.16.1)

It is difficult to be precise because we simply do not have accurate statistics, but it seems very likely that the city of Athens itself (not including Peiraieus; there were some three miles of open fields between the two) contained no more than a fifth of the total population of the Athenian *polis*, perhaps 50,000 people in all. Most Athenians made their living from the land, or from trades associated with its produce.

How Attica was governed before Solon's time is far from clear in detail, though we can trace the main outlines. Athenian tradition refers to a period of monarchy followed by rule by leading noble families through the Council of the Areopagos (the 'Hill of Ares' some 300 metres west of the Athenian Acropolis, where the Council met – see Map 4) with officers called generically 'arkhons' (simply 'rulers'). To put dates to this process is difficult, but it seems likely that by about 700 the kings had gone and that the Council of the Areopagos (appointed by the powerful noble families from their own members) was effectively in charge.

In the early days after the removal of the monarchy there were apparently three arkhons, the Basileus ('king') in charge of religious and state rituals, the Polemarch in charge of war, and one called simply the arkhon, who had general administrative duties and was probably a slightly later invention than the other two, though he was actually the most powerful and the period of his office (later restricted to one year only) was named after him (he is therefore often referred to as the eponymous arkhon). Then six more arkhons were added, called *thesmothetai* ('lawsetters'), who were in some way in charge of the state's laws, though details remain obscure. By the time these latter were added the period of office of the arkhons had been reduced from ten years to an annual appointment, and it seems to have become established practice that ex-arkhons automatically entered the Areopagos. They were undoubtedly the chief officers of the state, aided by a collection of minor officials mainly for financial matters, and responsible perhaps to the Council of the Areopagos, but even this seems in no way to have been formalised. We have no knowledge of the process by which arkhons were appointed, except that they were selected from those of noble birth and considerable wealth. The process was certainly entirely within the hands of the noble families.

The population of Attica was divided amongst the four 'Ionic tribes' (supposedly founded by Ion, ancestor of all Ionian Greeks), ancient groupings of noble families to which every citizen belonged either as a member of one of the noble families or as a retainer. The tribes were the basis of military organisation and also of some religious and financial functions. Each was divided into three *trittyes* ('threesomes'; singular *trittys*), and each *trittys* into four *naukrariai* (a word of doubtful origin. It may mean 'ships' captaincies', which would probably indicate that originally a *naukraria* was responsible for providing a ship but had then taken on other functions; but it may mean 'households', perhaps in the sense of 'extended families'.) Within each tribe there were also several *phratriai* (brotherhoods), each headed by one of the noble families, though how these fitted with *trittyes* and *naukrariai* is not clear. These *phratriai* were essentially social and religious groupings, and each had its own cult centre dedicated to the god or hero who was regarded as the patron of the *phratria*. The *phratriai* also had an important political role in that registration in a *phratria* was proof of citizenship; and it seems that the noble family which headed the *phratria* decided who was registered and who was not.

During the seventh century there seems also to have been an assembly of citizens, probably of those able to provide their own armour and fight as hoplites, but how it was consulted and about what is quite obscure. There seems little doubt that it was the arkhons, with the advice of the Areopagos, who really ran the state. As far as the mass of the people were concerned, they were all attached, mostly as tenant farmers, to one or other of the noble families and hence to one of the four tribes, but had no say in government at all.

An incident in 632 (or thereabouts) and its sequel, however, shows that there were tensions within the Athenian ruling class. The incident involved a man called Kylon, a member of one of the aristocratic families of Athens, who was married to the daughter of Theagenes, the tyrant of Megara, some thirty miles west of Athens on the Saronic Gulf. With the help of his father-in-law and his friends within Athens Kylon tried to make himself tyrant of Athens. He and his associates (who included a small force from Megara) occupied the Acropolis – but that was as far as they got. Nobody else supported the attempted coup, and Kylon and his men were besieged on the Acropolis. Kylon himself apparently escaped (though the accounts differ), but his supporters surrendered. They were given an assurance that they would not be killed, but despite the fact that some at least took sanctuary at altars near the Acropolis they were all massacred on the instructions of the arkhons, or perhaps more specifically of the eponymous arkhon, Megakles, a member of the Alkmeonid family (of which we shall hear a lot more). At the time that seemed to be the end of the matter; what appears to have been a pretty incompetent attempt at a coup by one aristocratic group had failed miserably and the perpetrators had been duly punished. But about thirty years later there was an interesting sequel. By this time Kylon's family seems to have gained much more influence, and accused the Alkmeonids of sacrilege for having massacred men who were taking sanctuary in the attempted coup of 632. The whole family of the Alkmeonids was thrown out of Athens, and even the bones of their ancestors were dug up and thrown out of the country. These Alkmeonids were evidently disliked by the rest of the aristocracy, and this was a convenient way of getting rid of them.

Kylon's conspiracy has been seen by some as evidence of discontent by the mass of the population, but the evidence we have does not support this. There may well have been discontent (we shall see that there certainly was a few years later), but if there was, few people saw Kylon as the solution to their problems.

By the late seventh century, however, clear signs of problems do begin to emerge. Around 621 the laws of Athens were codified by a certain Drakon (his name is all we know about him). They were notoriously harsh, imposing the death penalty for most offences. Rather oddly, the only detailed provision from Drakon's laws that we possess (in a copy from the late fifth century) seems quite lenient; in cases of unpremeditated killing it prescribes exile for the guilty party. It has been suggested that this provision reflects the violent feuding which was going on amongst the noble families, and was an attempt to remove out

9

of Attica those from the noble families guilty of mob violence, without incurring the death penalty which would probably result in yet more revenge killings. Whatever the full details of Drakon's code of laws, it seems it was a clear expression of the power of the aristocracy over everybody else.

Athens in the seventh century, then, was firmly governed by the aristocracy through the arkhons backed by the Council of the Areopagos. The various noble families were feuding amongst themselves, with the Alkmeonids apparently disliked by all the other families. They were exiled around 600 as we have seen, but they were soon to be back.

The evidence for social conditions at this period comes almost entirely from accounts of Solon's legislation in 594 (or a little later; see below), but the problems Solon tried to solve must have been building up for some time. The greatest problem was for those working on the land. Many had become impoverished through the system of *hektemorioi*, who were tenant farmers paying one-sixth of their produce to the landowner. The system almost certainly originated from the transfer of the land of owner farmers under some kind of mortgage to rich creditors as a result of debt. The *hektemorioi* then agreed to pay as rent one-sixth of their produce to the land owner, and markers were fixed in the ground to indicate that the land was held in this fashion. In the latter part of the seventh century many *hektemorioi* had found themselves unable to pay the sixth part to the landowner, and had been forced to sell their families and themselves as slaves to the landowner. By about 600 the situation was one of seething unrest. Elsewhere in Greece during the previous hundred years or so many cities had experienced revolutions and the emergence of a tyrant in very similar circumstances. The noble families of Athens were at least well aware of this possibility, and feared that one family might try to gain support from impoverished farmers and other groups by offering some alleviation from their poverty. It could well be that this is just what the Alkmeonid family were trying to do, and that it was this that led to their exile around 600 on the belated charge of sacrilege over the Kylon affair. It may also have occurred to the noble families that a state with a large population of disaffected peasants and feuds amongst the noble families themselves would find it difficult to recruit a unified army in time of need; and Megara, the neighbouring state to the west, was none too friendly and appears at this time to have occupied the island of Salamis, only a mile away from the shores of Attica. The political situation in Attica was fast becoming explosive. A solution was needed, and the noble families were almost ready to admit it.

Solon's reforms

Solon was an aristocrat, supposedly descended from one of the kings of Athens, but what wealth he had (it was said to be moderate) came from trade and not from land, which distanced him somewhat from the noble families. He had acquired a high reputation for his good sense and moderation, and particularly for his independence from the feuding landowning families. He was also a poet, and we have the advantage of still possessing some of his poetry (rather more than 200 lines), much of which is concerned with the politics of his day and particularly with his own reforms, which gives us an invaluable insight into his thinking – or rather as much of it as he was prepared to put into writing. With his experience through trade of the wider Greek world, and probably beyond, Solon must have been well aware how economically backward Athens was.

In 594 Solon was appointed arkhon, and either then or more probably at a later date, perhaps in the 570s, he was given a special commission to try to resolve the economic and political problems of the state, with the assurance of the Areopagos that his reforms would be accepted for ten years. It was a massive and unenviable task; of one thing he could be sure – he could not please everybody. He tackled the problems on two fronts, firstly through a series of economic reforms, and secondly through substantial revisions to the constitution.

As an economic package these reforms (see p. 12) made good sense. They were a well-considered attempt to increase the general productivity of Athens by freeing farmers from the burden of accumulated debt, ensuring a reasonable supply of local produce and stimulating trade, in particular the export of olive oil of which Athens could produce a considerable surplus. But the very fact that these reforms were needed so badly illustrates the hold the noble landowning families had over the state – and trade had hardly been on their agenda.

Solon's economic reforms

- All debts were cancelled. This was, of course, an extremely radical measure, and must have cost most wealthy families dear, since they were the major lenders. This action was referred to as the *seisakhtheia*, 'shaking off of burdens'.

- Linked with this was the removal of the markers on the lands of the *hektemorioi* as a sign that the land was no longer mortgaged, but was returned to the farmer. Again, the wealthy suffered considerable loss of their arguably ill-gotten gains.

- In future there could be no enslavement for debt, or to put it another way loans could not be secured on the debtor's person. Moreover retrospective action was taken to free any Athenian who had been enslaved for debt, and some effort seems to have been made to free even those who had been sold abroad.

- No foodstuffs could be exported except olive oil (which Attica produced in abundance). The purpose of this was to prevent the export of foods which could fetch a higher price abroad than at home. The effect of such exports had been to keep prices up at home, as well as to create shortages.

- Weights and measures were reformed to the standards operating in Corinth and the cities of Euboea, which were economically in advance of Athens. This made trading with these and most other cities, which were already using Corinthian and Euboean measures, much easier, and this reform, if no others, must have been welcome to the trading community.

- Skilled craftsmen from abroad were encouraged to settle in Athens to ply their trade. Solon as a trader himself was well aware that Athens was economically backward, and this measure was designed to increase Athens' productivity quickly.

In reforming the constitution Solon saw it as essential to break the hold of the aristocratic families on the government of the state. So far the power of the arkhons, who were always chosen from members of the noble families and backed by the Areopagos, had been in effect absolute. Solon was intent on broadening the power structure of government, to include especially those who had substantial wealth and property (mostly from trade of various sorts) but who were not from the noble families. His own trading background no doubt influenced him in this direction, but the pressure for such a constitutional reform must have been building up for some time. As the basis for his new constitution Solon therefore established (or perhaps more accurately formalised) the following four property classes.

The Athenian property classes

- The *pentakosiomedimnoi*, '500 measure men', that is those who from their own estate produced annually at least 500 *medimnoi*, which was both a dry and a liquid measure, one *medimnos* being equivalent to about 38 kilograms (85 lbs) and about 50 litres (11 gallons). A man typically consumed about eight *medimnoi* of wheat per year, and a man, wife and three children about 25 *medimnoi*. One can add perhaps another ten or so *medimnoi* of other food and drink to make up the basic diet for a family. This means that 500 *medimnoi* were enough to feed about fifteen families, or 40–50 men. The *pentakosiomedimnoi* were therefore comfortably off, but at the lower end of the range and not tremendously wealthy. Probably all the independent males from the aristocratic families fell comfortably into this class; but so did quite a lot of non-aristocrats.

- The *hippeis*, 'horsemen, knights', who produced 300–500 *medimnoi*. The title doubtless reflected the ability to provide a horse and be a cavalryman in times of war, but Solon now converted the term into a clearly specified property qualification.

13

- The *zeugitai*, 'yoke-men', probably referring to men who were 'yoked' in pairs as fully armed infantrymen (*hoplitai*), and therefore in origin indicating the ability to pay for one's own armour as a hoplite, though the word might possibly originally mean those who could provide a yoked pair of oxen. The property qualification for *zeugitai* was 200–300 *medimnoi*.

- The *thetes*. The word originally meant a serf, a man bound to his master and to his land, but later the word referred to any hired labourer. In Solon's system it meant anyone who produced less than 200 *medimnoi* per year, and this class must have included at least half, and in Solon's time probably considerably more, of the total citizen population.

Solon then defined his new constitution in terms of these property classes.

The nine arkhons were retained, but election to the arkhonship was now open to anyone from the *pentakosiomedimnoi* class (perhaps also to *hippeis*, though the evidence is unclear). Though the noble families were undoubtedly within the *pentakosiomedimnoi* class, there was a considerable number of non-nobles now eligible for election. Since ex-arkhons still progressed automatically to membership of the Areopagos, this body would gradually begin to lose its exclusively aristocratic composition, and this was undoubtedly Solon's intention.

Other offices, which appear to have been mainly financial, were open to *pentakosiomedimnoi*, *hippeis*, and *zeugitai*, but not to *thetes*.

Solon is credited with the setting up of a new Council of 400, consisting of 100 members from each of the four tribes. The very existence of this Council has been much debated, but the tradition for its creation by Solon does seem strong, even though we hear nothing of its operation for the rest of the sixth century. We do not know how members of this Council were chosen, but it seems that it was made up of representatives of the upper three property classes. The Council appears to have had considerable powers, in particular acting as overseer of all state officers and setting the agenda for the Assembly (see below). The Council of

400 thus took over many of the powers which the Areopagos had previously exercised. In practice this may not have been quite such a radical change as might appear. Even though the tribal organisation on which the new Council was based is far from clear, it must have been dominated by the noble families within each tribe, and though they could probably not fill the new Council with their own members (we are not even sure of that!), their influence must still have been considerable. It is surely significant that Kleisthenes in 508/7 deliberately dismantled this tribal structure in his new constitution, and this could indeed be seen as a powerful argument for the existence at the time of the tribally based Council of 400.

The Assembly was now open to all four property classes, that is to all male citizens. This sounds like a very democratic move, but one must bear in mind that its agenda was apparently set entirely by the Council of 400. In effect the political powers of the Assembly seem to have remained very restricted, but they do seem to have included some powers of scrutiny over the actions of the officers of the state.

In the administration of justice Solon carried out a thoroughly radical reform. A new court system was introduced in which *all* property classes were included as jurors, and any citizen could appeal to these new courts against the decision of one of the arkhons. The new courts did not replace the legal function of the arkhons, but they were a democratic check on their powers. These courts (called *heliaia*) may have been in practice divisions of the Assembly, or even the whole Assembly meeting as a court. One suspects that this measure may reflect great popular discontent with the law after the publication of Drakon's code. Solon therefore put the final power in the administration of justice into the hands of a cross-section of the whole citizen population – a very astute move, since it gave all citizens a role within the state administration without including all in policy making.

And what about the Council of the Areopagos? Certainly its power was reduced, but its status as an august body of elder statesmen may even have been enhanced by the fact that its membership was now taken from a broader base of very able men. It retained the power to try cases of homicide, and Solon also gave it the formal task of supervising the laws and the constitution, which was probably a more important role than has sometimes been assumed, since it must have had powers to carry this out and therefore must at least have had some power of veto over the actions of officers and other bodies; but we know little of how all this worked.

Solon put forward all his proposals at a public meeting, probably a special meeting of the Assembly (in its old form), and they were accepted. He had been assured by the Areopagos, as we have seen above, that his reforms, whatever they were, would be accepted for ten years; they were maybe not too pleased with the outcome, but we hear of no attempt to go back on their word. Solon himself left the country and travelled in Egypt and Asia Minor. He later wrote of his reforms:

> To the people I gave such status as is sufficient,
> Neither depriving them of honour nor offering them
> too much.
> The powerful who are envied because of their wealth
> I protected from all mistreatment.
> I took my stand offering a strong shield for both sides,
> Allowing neither side to dominate unjustly.
>
> (Solon, fragment 5 as in West 1992)

This is a fair assessment of his achievements.

Solon's reputation thereafter was great and he was regarded as one of the 'Seven Sages' of the Greek world. In Athens much was later attributed to him which he did not do, and for this reason (among others) the reconstruction of his reforms is still the subject of much debate. Nevertheless, Solon's reputation must have been based on some quite drastic changes to the law and constitution of Athens, and the reconstruction given above represents a general consensus of ancient and modern views.

But despite his later reputation Solon's reforms did not resolve all the problems as he had hoped. Unfortunately the rivalry and wrangling among the noble families continued (it is difficult to see how Solon could have stopped this). Although debts were cancelled by Solon's laws, many farmers quickly found themselves in debt again because they did not possess enough capital to see them through a farming year and they had to borrow again. Though they could not be enslaved (and that was indeed a great step forward), they were still bound to their aristocratic (and doubtless other) creditors by constant debt.

In the years following Solon's reforms there are clear signs of conflict; on two occasions in the next ten years an arkhon was not appointed (presumably because the various factions could not agree on a suitable candidate for this powerful position), and then a few years later a certain Damasias refused to lay down the arkhonship after the statutory year, perhaps intending to make himself tyrant. There was considerable turmoil, not because Solon's reforms were in themselves unworkable but because the most powerful noble families continued to contend amongst themselves for control of the system.

The tyranny of Peisistratos and Hippias

One important factor was that the Alkmeonids were back home again after their exile. We do not know when they returned, but they are not mentioned at all in the context of Solon's reforms, so presumably they were not in Athens at that time (they were not the sort of people to remain unmentioned at such a crisis if they had been in Athens!), but they must have come home soon afterwards. And it was not long before three new groupings of noble families emerged, those of 'the coast' (the south-west coast of Attica) headed by the Alkmeonids, those of 'the plain' (Athens itself and the plain to the north) probably led by the Boutadai family, and those 'beyond the hills' (the east coast region of Attica) now led by Peisistratos, who had estates around Brauron (see Map 2) on the east coast and whose family claimed to be descended from the royal family of Pylos on the west coast of the Peloponnese, whose most famous member was Nestor, king of Pylos during the Trojan War. Peisistratos was, or at least had been, a friend of Solon's (their mothers were cousins). It is interesting to note that these groupings do not seem to have any connection with the tribal divisions; land ownership and regional family alliances were the driving forces of this new geographical grouping, and perhaps the old Ionic tribes were already becoming politically less significant.

Peisistratos proved to be the most determined of the factional leaders. Between 560 and 546 he took over Athens as tyrant three times, once (the second time) in a brief alliance with the Alkmeonids (he married the daughter of Megakles, the head of the family). Twice his opponents, who each time included the Alkmeonids (the marriage alliance did not last long!), threw him out, but the third time he returned with a considerable army of mercenaries and with the backing of Thebes, Eretria on the island of Euboea, and the island of Naxos (see Map 1), as well as much popular support from the hill farmers of his home area in east Attica, and established himself firmly as the tyrant of Athens, driving the Alkmeonids into exile yet again. He remained tyrant until his death in 527 when he was well into his seventies.

So for nearly twenty years Peisistratos controlled Athens. Whereas most tyrants of Greek cities gained a reputation for brutality and oppression, Peisistratos was remembered with great admiration, and he does seem to have done a good job of bringing stability and prosperity to Athens. In fact he left Solon's constitution intact (there is a tradition that Solon, who had returned to Athens some time before, worked with Peisistratos early in his tyranny; he must have been a very old man!). Peisistratos simply made sure that his own men always held the positions of power, in particular the arkhonship, which of course led to membership of the Areopagos, so that after twenty years this body was dominated by his own nominees. Presumably he controlled the Council of 400 in a similar way, though in fact we hear nothing of it under Peisistratos. Nevertheless, he was always anxious to preserve the constitutional niceties of Solon's reforms; they served his purposes well, and there was no need to change them. The only reform we hear of that in any way added to Solon's was his introduction of 'deme-judges' to try cases of local disputes, which doubtless replaced the informal legal authority of the local noble family.

Much of Peisistratos' reputation rested on his successful resolution of the problems which Solon's measures had left unresolved. Firstly, he prevented the old inter-faction strife by removing the Alkmeonids (who were always seen as trouble-makers by anyone who was not an Alkmeonid), together with a few other dissident families, from Attica. And secondly, he took action to make the economic position of small farmers, who were among those supporting him, more secure. This he did by offering them state loans, which were paid for out of a 10 per cent tax on all produce. In effect this measure transferred some of the profits of the more wealthy farmers to aid the poorer ones, though even the poorer ones contributed. It also kept poorer farmers out of the hands of extortionate money lenders. He also encouraged the planting of olive trees all over Attica. Olives do

18

well in Attica (olive oil was the one product Solon had excluded from his export ban), and this measure encouraged investment in olives as an export trade, perhaps as Solon had intended. It is doubtless not insignificant that the period of Peisistratos' tyranny also saw the height of Athenian black figure pottery. Both in the production of the pottery and in the artistry of the decoration Athenian vases now outclassed any others – a clear sign of prosperity and artistic confidence.

Under Peisistratos Athens was both prosperous and politically stable. Though constitutionally he did very little, Peisistratos did show that Solon's reforms could work – provided the aristocratic clans were not jostling for power – and this was an important message for the future. Unfortunately his sons were not of the same calibre. When he died in 527 the elder son Hippias stepped into his father's role, aided by his younger brothers Hipparkhos and Thettalos, both of whom spent most of their time as the rich playboys of Athenian society. We have little information about events until 514, but an inscription shows that Kleisthenes, son of Megakles and now head of the Alkmeonids, was arkhon in 525. The family must have returned on Peisistratos' death (or maybe before) and must presumably have come to some kind of arrangement with the Peisistratids. But before 514 they had gone off yet again into exile and began to plan to remove Hippias from Athens. For those who are counting, this was the third (and not yet the last) recorded exile of the Alkmeonids.

In the summer of 514 Hipparkhos was assassinated at the Panathenaic Festival by Harmodios and Aristogeiton, two young aristocrats. Their intention was to kill Hippias as well, but the plot went wrong. Harmodios was killed on the spot by Hipparkhos' bodyguards and Aristogeiton was arrested and later executed. If the plot was really intended to get rid of the tyranny it clearly failed; but Thucydides' version of the events (6.53–60) presents quite a different motive for the assassination. Harmodios and Aristogeiton were apparently lovers, and Hipparkhos had tried to seduce Harmodios. Having failed he insulted Harmodios' sister by saying she was unworthy to carry a basket in the Panathenaic procession (perhaps a slur on her virginity). Harmodios and Aristogeiton therefore decided, with some accomplices, to kill both Hippias and Hipparkhos. But even if we accept Thucydides' account (and one must

19

suspect that at least some of those involved had political motives), the two assassins were immediately hailed as tyrant-slayers, and later traditions regarded them as the ones who signalled the end of Hippias' tyranny.

In fact it took a lot more effort to unseat Hippias. The assassination of his brother made him understandably nervous, and for the next four years his regime became extremely oppress-ive. But meanwhile the Alkmeonids, in exile probably in nearby Boeotia, were planning his downfall. They got the contract to rebuild the temple of Apollo at Delphi, seat of the famous oracle, and did the job in splendid fashion, using Parian marble where the contract specified limestone. They were then able to persuade the oracle (or more probably the priests who inter-preted the ecstatic utterances of the old woman prophetess) to instruct any Spartan visitor to the oracle to 'free Athens'. Sparta was still governed by an ancient system in which *two* kings and a small council of aristocratic elders ruled the state, and they were in general supporters of aristocratic governments else-where, though they had been on friendly terms with the Peisis-tratid family. But they were apparently persuaded by the oracle and sent one of the kings, Kleomenes, to invade Athens, sup-ported of course by the Alkmeonids. In fact the Spartans may have been far more influenced by the fact that Hippias had recently made an alliance with Argos, the long-standing enemies of Sparta, and they were therefore happy to support the Alk-meonids, who they probably thought would set up the sort of aristocratic government they could do business with. With little bloodshed Hippias was driven out of Athens and fled to Sigeion on the north-west coast of Asia Minor (close to the site of Troy), which had been established by Athenian settlers about a hun-dred years before and with which his family had strong con-nections. From there he later went to the court of the Persian king Darius, who he thought would help him to regain his position in Athens.

The Alkmeonids, however, were far from being universally welcomed in Athens, and it looked for a while as if Athens would revert to the factional battles so common before Peisis-tratos. Kleisthenes was immediately opposed by Isagoras, a leading member of one of the prominent aristocratic families, though we do not know which one. Isagoras got himself appointed arkhon for 508, but it soon became apparent that he was no match for the Alkmeonids, who were gaining widespread popular support among the poorer Athenians. However, Isagoras happened to have ties of friendship with the Spartan king Kleomenes, and he therefore sought Kleomenes' help against the Alkmeonids – whom Kleomenes had just helped to return from exile! Kleomenes had perhaps by this time got wind of Kleisthenes' popular support and the likely direction of his reforming ideas, and thought that Isagoras was now the man to back. He therefore sent a small force to Athens to help him. With this Spartan support Isagoras now exiled the Alkmeonids (for the fourth time in the last hundred years), together with many other families, and tried to dismantle the constitution and set up a council of his own supporters. This created a riot in Athens, and Isagoras and his Spartan supporters found themselves besieged on the Acropolis by the angry populace, who saw all that had been gained by Solon's reforms fast disappearing. After a two-day siege Kleomenes realised he was on the losing side and a truce was agreed allowing all the Spartans to leave; but Isagoras' Athenian supporters were arrested and then executed, though Isagoras himself escaped with the Spartan contingent. The Alkmeonids and all others exiled by Isagoras were promptly recalled. Kleisthenes, now firmly in control, carried out a constitutional reform which introduced to Athens the most radical democracy in the ancient world.

3

The democratic system: Kleisthenes' reforms

The details of how Kleisthenes actually carried out his reforms of the constitution are unclear. He appears not to have held any formal office (certainly not the arkhonship), but he may possibly have been given a special commission to revise the constitution after the departure of Isagoras. The date usually given for Kleisthenes' reforms is 508/7, but there is strong evidence that the basic system took at least two or three years to set up, presumably with some kind of interim government operating during this period.

Kleisthenes and the Alkmeonids had regained their position in Athens with the support of the *demos*, the non-aristocratic farmers and craftsmen, who were by now thoroughly disillusioned with aristocratic control of the state. The *demos* probably constituted over 90 per cent of the population, though they did not all necessarily support Kleisthenes; many may have been just as suspicious of the Alkmeonids as they were of the other aristocratic clans. We know nothing of what negotiations took place between Kleisthenes and representatives of the *demos*, but there surely must have been some. Whatever the details, Kleisthenes can have been in no doubt that his reforms must gain the support of the majority of the *demos* by giving them real powers in the government of the state. He must quickly have realised, whether he liked it or not, that this meant he had somehow to break the hold of the aristocratic families on the whole political system. Their power bases were essentially threefold: firstly, their hold on their estates and on those who lived on them, typified earlier by the alliances of 'the coast', 'the plain', and 'beyond the hills'; secondly, the old tribal loyalties of the four Ionic tribes acknowledged in Solon's Council of 400 and still the basis of military and financial organisation; and thirdly, the arkhonship and the Areopagos, which were still largely dominated by aristocrats. His reforms had to satisfy the *demos* that they and not the aristocratic clans were in power, and would remain so. But we can detect clear signs of compromise and manoeuvring. As we shall see, the arkhonship and the Areopagos were to remain apparently intact; and Kleisthenes was certainly not averse to benefiting his Alkmeonid clan at the expense of other clans as far as he could in the reform process.

The new tribes

Kleisthenes simply abandoned the old Ionic tribes as the basis for any political activity; he did not in fact try to dissolve them, since they had certain social and cult functions which he saw no reason to tamper with, but they now became politically and constitutionally irrelevant. But because of the regional alliances of the aristocratic clans he no doubt felt he could not replace the old tribes by a simple geographical pattern of 'counties', 'departments' or 'cantons', which would quickly become dominated by one or more of the aristocratic clans. He therefore devised a much more complex system in which he created ten new tribes, each consisting of a section of the city of Athens, a section of the coastal area, and a section of the inland region. The system must have appeared just as complicated to the population of Attica in 508/7 as it does to us now, and its acceptance must indicate that there was general consensus that something like this was necessary to prevent a return to the aristocratic factional in-fighting which had dominated the politics of the previous two centuries.

The organisation of the ten new tribes was the foundation of virtually the whole of political life at the level of the state (we shall consider late, pp. 47–9, the political life of the individual demes) under the new democracy, and it is therefore essential to an understanding of the working of the democracy to consider

23

in some detail how these tribes were constituted. Though we do not possess all the details, a fairly accurate picture can now be built up, using literary evidence (limited in amount and often much later than the fifth century BC, but still invaluable), inscriptions found in Athens and Attica (more are still being found), and archaeological evidence for the geography and settlement patterns of Attica in classical times.

Map 2 shows how Kleisthenes divided Attica into three basic areas, the city, the coast, and inland. The 'city' actually consisted of Athens itself, the port of Peiraieus, and a considerable area of land (mostly good farmland) around these, including some thirty miles of coast. This was presumably designed to increase the population of this 'city' sector to something approaching each of the other two, and even then it seems that the city sector was the smallest in population of the three; most Athenians still lived in the 'country'. Each of these sectors was then divided into ten sections, each called a *trittys* (the word had in fact been used previously to describe a third part of one of the old Ionic tribes, so people were familiar with its use as a political division). The meaning 'threesome' was still relevant, since it was three of these sections (one each from the city, the coast and inland) which made up one of the ten new tribes (see Map 3). There were therefore in total thirty of these *trittyes* in the whole of the state: ten in the city, ten on the coast, and ten inland. The *trittyes* mostly consisted of groups of 'demes', which were villages (or clusters of villages and hamlets) in the rural areas and what we would term wards in the city. The villages, hamlets and city wards were of course already there; Kleisthenes decided which were to be the focal points of the new 'demes' and then clustered them into the new *trittyes*. We know fairly certainly that there were 139 demes in the whole state, so the average number of demes to a *trittys* was four or five. But in practice the *trittyes* varied considerably in the number of demes they contained, from just one deme in several cases (probably five instances) to eight or nine demes in a few *trittyes*, and this reflected the great variation in population of the demes. Every male citizen on reaching the age of 18 was now to be registered in his deme. It was this registration which confirmed his citizenship, and even if he later moved to another part of Attica he and his descendants after him remained members of the deme in which he first registered in 508/7. Through the deme he was a member of the *trittys*, and hence a member of one of the ten tribes. This new form of registration replaced as proof of citizenship registration with a *phratria*, which had never been open to all free males but was controlled by the aristocratic family which headed the *phratria*. The *phratriai* continued, but had no formal political role. (Appendix 1 contains a complete list of all tribes, divided into *trittyes* and demes. The location of all the *trittyes* can be seen on Map 3.)

The actual allocation process by which the thirty *trittyes* were arranged into the ten new tribes is still unclear, even though we know the outcome quite well. The *Athenaion Politeia* (21.4) says that the *trittyes* were assigned to tribes by lot, and some modern scholars defend this view. Some, however, think it more likely that Kleisthenes (or a commission set up to carry out the reforms) planned carefully which *trittyes* were put together to form each tribe. There are two main reasons for taking this view. The first is that the tribes needed to be closely comparable in size of population (all forms of political and military organisation within the state resulting from the reforms seem to have assumed this), and the *trittyes* themselves were definitely not so. Even though a random combination of any three *trittyes* for each tribe would on the whole produce tribes which were roughly comparable in size, there was of course a chance that three smaller *trittyes* (or bigger ones) could emerge from a random choice as one tribe and thus vitiate the system, or at least make it patently unbalanced. A planned approach seems more likely to have been acceptable. The second reason is that there is some evidence that the geographical organisation of *trittyes* into tribes favoured the Alkmeonids, and this is not likely to be the result of chance.

We cannot as yet produce a complete map of Attica showing every deme because the location of some demes is still not known, but the general pattern is clear. At first sight the distribution pattern may well appear to be as one would expect from a random selection of *trittyes* to form tribes (though allowing, perhaps, for some balancing of size to create more or less equal tribes, as indicated above), and may therefore seem to support the statement quoted above from the *Athenaion Politeia*. But when we look at the geographical areas known to be under the influence of the Alkmeonids an interesting pattern emerges. The Alkmeonid estates and areas of influence were located in the region to the south of Athens, from Peiraieus down the coast of the Saronic Gulf, probably reaching within a few miles of Cape Sounion, the area comprising the old definition of 'the coast'. If we look at the *trittyes* in this area (see Map 3) we find that much of the territory to the south of the city (the northern end of the Alkmeonid influence) is allocated to *trittyes* from tribes I, VII and X – and so are the *trittyes* in the coastal strip which forms the rest of the Alkmeonid territory, down to near Cape Sounion. The Alkmeonids therefore in effect controlled these three tribes, since roughly two-thirds of each tribe was within their territory. Actually the inland *trittyes* of all three of these tribes were also fairly close to Athens, though we do not know if this is significant or not. Unfortunately we do not know the home areas of enough of the other aristocratic families to see if the allocation of *trittyes* to tribes deliberately linked them with two other *trittyes* in each tribe which were from areas outside their control and thus ensured that other families could not influence a majority in any tribe. Nor do we know if deals were done with some aristocratic clans, or even other groupings, to ensure their support. However, the clustering of *trittyes* of tribes II, III, V and IX on the east coast does look suspiciously like a deliberate configuration. This is in fact the old region 'beyond the hills', the domain of the Peisistratids! Did Kleisthenes even do a deal with the remnant of the Peisistratids? There were certainly rumours at the time of the battle of Marathon in 490 that the Alkmeonids were still in contact with Hippias and his Persian friends (see Herodotus 6.115 and 121 ff.; he did not believe the rumours, but they were there). Or perhaps Kleisthenes did a deal with the new owners of the Peisistratid estates (or most of the estates; we know that some of the family did stay after Hippias' departure), since these new owners must have been grateful to Kleisthenes for their new properties. It is interesting to note that Herodotus records (6.121) that a certain Kallias had previously bought the estates of Peisistratos at the time when he was exiled from Athens (this must have been in the 550s), and we know that this Kallias came from the same city deme, Alopeke, as Kleisthenes' family. Did the descendants of Kallias, who we know were still living near Kleisthenes' family in Alopeke in 508, buy the Peisistratid estates back again sfter Hippias' departure? It looks as if there may be more to all this than we can prove for certain. Whatever the details, Kleisthenes may have done deals both with the remaining Peisistratids and with the new owners of these east coast estates. By these means he may have hoped to be able to influence a majority (two-thirds) of the *trittyes* of *seven* tribes (I, VII and X, and II, III, V and IX) – but one has to admit that the evidence is circumstantial. Nevertheless, the suspicion remains that the allocation of *trittyes* to tribes was quite a subtle game, and Kleisthenes may well have played it as far as he could.

The new tribes had considerable business to transact or to oversee, in particular the appointment of a considerable number of officers, for the *Boule* (see the following section) and for the numerous committees of magistrates, all of which had equal membership from each tribe. The citizens forming a tribe therefore had to meet fairly regularly in Athens. These tribal assemblies were probably dominated by members from the city demes, and though this was maybe not a big issue for members from the coastal and inland demes since the tribal assemblies were not in any sense policy-making bodies, we do see some effects in the appointment of generals, as will be noted below.

The Council of 500 (the *Boule*)

This new council was at the heart of the new democracy, though it should be stressed straight away that its powers were executive; it did not itself make policy: that was the job of the Assembly, which was open to all citizens over the age of 20 (see pp. 31–3). Nevertheless, it was the Council of 500 which in effect ran the state, carrying out the policies of the Assembly.

The *Boule* consisted of 500 citizens over the age of 30, fifty from each of the ten tribes. The fifty members from each tribe were distributed unevenly across the three *trittyes*, since it was at deme level that the allocations of *Boule* members were made, the number reflecting the citizen population of each deme (see Appendix 1 for the number of *Boule* members from each deme and *trittys*). Many smaller demes (about forty) had only one member of the *Boule*, but eight had ten or more, and the biggest deme (Akharnai, about seven miles north of Athens, which was also a *trittys* in itself) had twenty-two. But in each tribe the total *Boule* members from the three *trittyes* was always fifty. It is interesting to note that if we calculate the total of *Boule* members from the city, the coast, and inland *trittyes* we get the

27

following figures (within two or three, since in some demes numbers varied slightly; see Appendix 1):

City: 130
Coast: 196
Inland: 174

As we have noted before, it appears that the city, even on the extended definition used by Kleisthenes, was smaller in population than each of the other two sections. Those who lived in Athens itself apparently constituted no more than a fifth of the total population of the state, even including the metics (foreigners resident in Athens). In fact, within the geographical area covered by Kleisthenes' 'City', the actual city of Athens within the walls provided only twenty-eight *Boule* members, and the urban area immediately outside the walls provided a further twenty-nine; so, of the 130 *Boule* members from the 'City', only fifty-seven came from the urban area of Athens itself, and the remaining seventy-three came from the port of Peiraieus (with ten *Boule* members) and the relatively rural areas which made up the rest of the 'City' region. From these figures it seems that the population of the urban area of Athens (that is, those living within and just outside the walls), including metics and slaves, was probably around 50,000, about 20 per cent of the total population of the state, but containing only some 12 per cent (if *Boule* members are a fair guide to citizen numbers, and they probably are) of the total citizen population; the city of Athens had a much higher than average number of non-citizens, since it contained many of the metics and most probably a considerable concentration of slaves. It is indeed true that Athens was essentially a rural state.

The term of office for the *Boule* was one year, as it was for nearly all other offices of the state, beginning around midsummer. The same person could not be a member of the *Boule* in two consecutive years, and could only be a member twice in a lifetime.

Kleisthenes did not, however, make membership of the *Boule* open to all citizens, but only to those whose property qualification put them in the *zeugitai* class (possessing an annual income of at least 200 *medimnoi*) or above. The *thetes* class, who constituted probably well over a half of the citizen popu-

28

lation, were thus excluded from the *Boule*, just as they had been excluded from Solon's Council of 400.

This gives rise to a nice calculation, which presumably Kleisthenes must have done. The *Boule* required 500 members from the *zeugitai* class and above each year, and individuals could be members of the *Boule* only twice in a lifetime. If we assume that the average life expectancy of those aged 30 was a further thirty years, then it might be assumed that an individual would be eligible for membership of the *Boule* on average once every fifteen years. Therefore, when the new system was fully operational, the state needed at least 7,500 citizens of *zeugitai* class or above aged over 30 (there may, of course, have been some who did not wish to serve on the *Boule*) in order to ensure that the *Boule* could be manned each year. If we extrapolate this figure to cover those citizens between the ages of 20 and 30, we have a minimum of about 10,000 citizens of *zeugitai* class and above. There are indications that the total adult citizen population was about 30,000, so the figures do seem to fit. If we assume that about 10,000–15,000 were of *zeugitai* class or above and the rest were *thetes* we shall probably not be far out.

Members of the *Boule* had certain privileges. They were not required to do military service during their year of office, they had specially reserved seats at state functions (including the drama festivals), and they wore a crown of myrtle (as did other officers of the state) as a mark of office. But the duties were quite onerous. There were meetings of the *Boule* in the *bouleuterion* (council chamber) in the *agora* in Athens every day except on festival days and on a few days of ill omen. Some members doubtless did not attend all the meetings, especially if they lived some distance from Athens, but too frequent absence could lead to criticism. There were also committees of the *Boule* and numerous state functions that members were expected to attend.

In order to ensure a fair distribution of work and to provide a constant administrative presence, especially important for emergencies, the fifty *Boule* members from each tribe took it in turns to act as a standing committee (*prytaneis*) of the *Boule* for a period of thirty-six days. The order in which the tribes served as the *prytaneis* was established by lot at the beginning of each 'prytany' period. All fifty members of the *prytaneis* on duty were housed and fed in the *tholos*, a building adjacent to the *bouleuterion*. Each day one of their number was chosen by lot as chairman, and he was required to stay in the *tholos* for the twenty-four hour period of his office. The chairman for the day presided over any meeting of the *Boule* held that day, and if there was a meeting of the Assembly that day (they were held about every nine days) he also presided over that. This must have been a formidable task, since there were typically about 5,000 people at a meeting of the Assembly. So the majority of the 500 *Boule* members could expect to be president of the *Boule* for a day, and around forty of them would preside at a meeting of the Assembly in the course of the year.

As the executive committee of the state the *Boule* had numerous functions. Perhaps its prime function, and the task which put great power in the hands of the *Boule*, was to prepare the agenda for all meetings of the Assembly, and this included draft proposals (called *probouleumata*), either in the form of recommendations or simply as open questions for the Assembly to decide on. The *Boule* also received all embassies to Athens, and decided whether they should have access to a meeting of the Assembly. Much of their work, however, was in implementing the policy of the Assembly, and in this area perhaps most of the work was concerned with the finance and organisation of public works and services, including military expenditure. In fact the *Boule* was the responsible body of the state in the implementation of all policies, even if there were other officers and committees (and there were plenty of both, as we shall see) who actually did the work.

The *Boule* was crucial to the working of the whole new democratic system, and it did of course contain members from every deme in Attica, but two further features are worth considering in a little more detail.

Firstly, its membership was very carefully vetted. Kleisthenes restricted its membership, as we have seen, to those of *zeugitai* status and above, probably arguing that these classes had a financial interest in good government and also provided hoplites for the armies (*thetes* did not, though they served in the fleet), whilst not representing the narrower interests of any one class or group. Anyone wishing to be put forward for membership of the *Boule* had to be approved first by his deme, and one can well imagine that demes were careful to select only those of known good sense who also had experience of local politics, and who were actually available to do the time-consuming job which demanded frequent attendance in Athens; and they probably favoured those who were well past 30. If there were more candidates than the deme's allocation of *Boule* members (and this was not necessarily the case), then lots were drawn (apparently in Athens) to decide on the successful candidates (see also later in this chapter, p.49). But even then the *Boule* in office had to check on each individual (the *dokimasia*, test) to ensure that all conditions were satisfied and the person selected was in no way disqualified.

Secondly, the annual change of membership, the *prytaneis* system, and the selection by lot of the president on a daily basis made it virtually impossible for any of the tribes (themselves, of course, from three different parts of Attica) or any other groupings of individuals to dominate the working of the *Boule*. This lack of permanence undoubtedly had its drawbacks, in particular the lack of opportunity to develop any depth of experience or expertise; but it did avoid the worst excesses of political factions and of aristocratic domination, and most Athenians were happy to accept the drawbacks.

The Assembly (*Ekklesia*)

The Assembly was the policy-making body of the state and consisted in principle of all male citizens over the age of 20. Most of the detailed evidence for the procedures of the Assembly comes from the surviving works of the orators of the fourth century (mainly Demosthenes) and from the *Athenaion Politeia*, which was apparently written about 330, and we cannot be sure how far this evidence is relevant in detail to procedures for the first hundred years or so of the democracy. The evidence which does exist from the earlier period does not conflict substantially with later procedures, however, and it is probably reasonable to assume that the general pattern of the Assembly's procedures was fairly stable.

Meetings of the Assembly were normally held four times in each prytany, forty times in a year. The meetings were usually held on the Pnyx, a gently sloping hill about 500 metres to the west of the Acropolis (see Map 4), which could accommodate around 6,000 people, though it seems likely that in the early decades of the democracy meetings were held in the market place (*agora*). Since the total number of citizens entitled to

31

attend the Assembly was in the region of 30,000, clearly most did not attend most of the time. The ones who did attend were presumably mainly those who lived in or near Athens. The east coast of Attica is a good two days' walk from Athens, and it was doubtless a rare event for someone from Marathon or Sounion to make the effort to come to an Assembly, unless he had to be in Athens for some other reason. But the evidence seems to suggest that there were usually enough at meetings to fill the Pnyx, more or less.

The agenda for every meeting of the Assembly was prepared by the *Boule*, or more precisely by the *prytaneis* for that period. The Assembly itself could decide that a particular item should be on a later agenda, but other than that the *Boule* controlled the agenda and published it several days before the meeting. The *prytaneis* for the period in which the meeting was held acted as a coordinating committee for the meeting, with the *Boule* president for that day as the chairman of the whole proceedings. Meetings started early in the morning soon after sunrise with prayers and the sacrifice of a pig, and usually ended by midday, though some meetings went on all day; at the trial of the generals after the battle of Arginoussai in 406 a vote was postponed because it was too dark to count the show of hands. The agendas for some meetings were at least in part pre-determined, especially for the *ekklesia kyria* ('main meeting'), which was one of the four in each prytany, at which there was always a vote of confidence in the officers of the state, together with items on the state's corn supply (the price of corn was determined by the state), on matters of defence, and on several legal matters such as the reporting of any confiscations of property by the state. Various members of the *prytaneis* put forward the *Boule*'s draft proposals (*probouleumata*) on each item, and then the official herald of the Assembly asked, 'Who wishes to speak?' Any member of the Assembly could then come to the platform and speak on that item. From a speech of Aeschines of around 340 we have some of the rules for speakers both in the *Boule* and in the Assembly:

Anyone addressing the *Boule* or the Assembly must keep to the matter in hand, must not deal with two separate matters together, and must not speak twice on the same matter at any one meeting. He must not engage in slanders or scurrility, or

32

interrupt others. He must speak only from the platform, and must not assault the presiding officer . . .

(Aeschines, Against Timarchus, 1.35)

Voting was done by a show of hands. If the vote was close any member of the Assembly could demand a recount. Four stone '*trittys* markers' have been discovered on or near the Pnyx, and it could be that these marked the places where members of each *trittys* sat in meetings of the Assembly; but some literary sources imply that people sat where they wished, so the matter remains unresolved.

Decisions of the Assembly were recorded and published, the more important ones carved on stone, and several have survived, though mostly in fragments. The opening phrases are fairly standardised, usually in the following form:

Resolution of the *Boule* and the People:
in the prytany of the tribe [name of tribe]
when . . . was secretary
and when . . . was chairman
. . . proposed this motion:

The Assembly was indeed the controlling body of the state. This is perhaps shown most clearly in the procedure known as *eisangelia*, which means denunciation on a charge of treason or conspiracy against the state. At each *ekklesia kyria*, held once in every prytany, any citizen could begin the procedure of *eisangelia* by denouncing any officer of the state, or even a private citizen, and for such a motion no *probouleuma* was required from the *Boule*. If the Assembly was convinced that there was a case to answer, it then decided whether to try the case at a special meeting of the Assembly itself (which it did in important cases) or to refer it to the courts. The notorious trial of the generals after the battle of Arginoussai in 406 was the result of an *eisangelia*, and shows the power of the Assembly, for good or ill, over the officers of the state.

The law courts (*Dikasteria*)

Since the time of Solon's reforms the administration of justice had been to a certain extent in the hands of courts (the *heliaia*) which contained all classes of citizen and to which any citizen could appeal against the decision of an arkhon. People had become used to the idea of cases being tried and penalties set by large numbers of their fellow citizens. It is therefore no surprise that Kleisthenes followed the principles established by Solon, but he refined the system considerably. It should be noted, though, that during the early fifth century the *dikasteria*, as they were known after Kleisthenes' reforms, remained in principle courts of appeal, cases being first referred to one of the arkhons or, in cases of robbery and certain other acts of violence, to the Eleven, who were annually appointed magistrates in charge of the state prison and of the 'police force' of 300 Scythian archers, with powers to fine and impose other punishments, even the death penalty, if the culprit was caught in the act. In the early decades of the fifth century the arkhons do seem to have retained some powers to judge cases, but the procedures are unclear.

Athens had no state legal service in the sense of paid professional judges, nor were there professional lawyers in anything like the modern sense. The different kinds of prosecutions will be discussed below (p.35), but in most actions the person making the accusation served a summons on the defendant to appear with him before the relevant arkhon on a stated day. If the defendant did not appear the accuser won his case by default; usually, of course, the defendant *did* appear. Then the arkhon heard evidence from both sides, took written statements and any relevant documentary evidence, and arranged for the case to be heard by a court. In court each party was allotted time to speak, and this was measured by a *klepsydra*, a water clock constructed from a large pot which allowed water to flow out at a fixed rate. Both accusers and defendants frequently made use of professional speech-writers, and it was normal procedure for defendants to bring along their wives and children to put on a show of poverty and weeping to excite the court's pity and leniency. After the speeches the members of the court ('dikasts' – see below for how they were selected) voted without any formal debate, placing a voting disc into 'guilty' or 'not guilty' urns. One might guess that finer points of law were hardly deciding factors in these courts, and impassioned speeches were more likely to win the day. The Athenian view seems simply to have been that large numbers of dikasts were less likely to get it wrong than small numbers of arkhons.

The six arkhons known as *thesmothetai* (law-setters) continued to be responsible for the organisation of the law courts as they probably had been since Solon's time, and they presided over several of the courts, but their term of office was restricted to one year. Prosecutions were brought either by the individual with a grievance (such cases were called *dikai*), or, in matters which were regarded as of public rather than private concern, by anyone who wished to do so (these cases were called *graphai*) – but in the latter kind of case there was a real risk to the accuser; if he withdrew the case before it came to court, or if at the trial he failed to gain at least a fifth of the votes of the court, then he was deprived of civic rights and fined 1,000 drachmas, which was about three years' pay for a craftsman. This was clearly designed as a deterrent against frivolous or malicious accusations. In the case of *dikai*, if the aggrieved party won the case he or his next of kin received compensation from the guilty party. In the case of *graphai*, if the defendant lost then he was fined (usually heavily), and the successful prosecutor received a substantial reward, which was enough to attract some unscrupulous people, despite the risk of losing their civic rights and 1,000 drachmas, to bring *graphai* prosecutions with the main intention of making a profit. Such prosecutors were called *sykophantai*, which literally appears to mean 'fig revealers', probably a reference to bringing prosecutions against those illegally exporting figs, which was prohibited by Solon's reforms. The *graphai* system was constantly open to this kind of abuse, and seems to have been much used for personal vendettas.

There must presumably have been some kind of local method of resolving minor disputes, probably within the deme. Peisistratos had introduced deme-judges, and perhaps these continued to be appointed. We have some details of a system of deme courts from the mid-fifth century onwards which will be mentioned later, but we have no record of what was happening in demes from Kleisthenes' time.

Under Kleisthenes' reforms each year 6,000 citizens aged 30 or over were chosen and registered as a pool of jurors. (Actually, since these jurors acted as both jurymen and judges, it is best to use the Greek word *dikastes*, or the anglicised form 'dikast'.) The 6,000 were chosen by lot from those willing to stand, 600 being selected from each of the new tribes. One might have guessed that most of those who put themselves forward were

35

from the city, but such evidence as we have seems to indicate that many were in fact from the coast and inland areas. They were on the whole middle-aged or elderly, since few in the 30–50 age range would have the time to sit regularly in the courts, and the majority (at least after the introduction of pay for dikasts around 451/0) seem to have been from the poorer end of the social spectrum. Each dikast received a 'ticket' (made of bronze during the mid-fourth century, but probably of wood in the fifth century) with his full name and an official stamp showing the owl of Athena. Many of the bronze variety have been found, often in graves; presumably in most of these cases the dead man was a dikast in the year he died and proudly had his dikast's ticket buried with him. Each year all the newly appointed dikasts attended a ceremony at which they took the 'Heliastic Oath', which may well date from Solon's time, with modifications to fit Kleisthenes' reforms. The wording was as follows:

> I shall vote according to the laws and the decrees passed by the Assembly and the *Boule*, but concerning things about which there are no laws I shall decide to the best of my judgement, without favour or enmity. I will vote only on the matters raised in the charge, and I will listen impartially to accusers and defenders alike.

Courts were held on all days except Assembly days and on festival days. This left around 200 working days. The size of the courts varied depending on the nature of the case. In the fourth century *dikai* cases involving sums of less than 1,000 drachmas were judged by a panel of 201 dikasts, and those of more than 1,000 drachmas by a panel of 401 dikasts; *graphai* cases were usually judged by panels of 501, but if the case was regarded as highly important multiples of 500 (+1) were used. All courts were held in or near the *agora* (see Map 4), though the exact location is still not clear; some buildings to the north-east of the *agora*, which were certainly courts at a later date, may be the site of the earlier courts as well.

In the fifth century the 6,000 dikasts were divided into ten sections, each containing 600 dikasts with 60 men from each of the ten tribes. Each of these ten sections was allocated for the year to one of ten courts, each presided over by one of the arkhons or in some cases by another magistrate. Each court dealt with a particular category of offence, for instance family and inheritance matters under the eponymous arkhon, and all affairs concerning metics and other non-Athenians under the Polemarch. On court days proceedings began at dawn, and for each court day a schedule of courts to be held and the number of dikasts required for each was published in advance. Those dikasts who wished to attend the court, if their allotted court was meeting that day, turned up and queued at the entrance, and in the fifth century the procedure seems to have been that the required number of dikasts was then let in on a 'first come, first served' basis, their identity tickets being checked or collected as they entered. This system was, of course, open to some abuse, since dikasts were attached to a particular court and could pretty well ensure being in court for a particular case if they were there early enough; and that meant that they could be bribed, and apparently were. From 403 onwards various reforms to the allocation system of dikasts to courts were carried out, and from about 370 the system was highly elaborate, with the use of random selection machines (a *kleroterion*), part of one of which has survived.

In Kleisthenes' reforms the dikasts were not paid; as we shall see, this was to come later.

The Athenian system of law courts is remarkable in many ways, not least for the sheer number of people regularly involved. The Athenians themselves regarded it as an essential part of their democracy. The law courts certainly played a dominant role in the life of the state, and were a way of life for many, perhaps most of the elderly citizens of Athens.

The generals (*strategoi*)

Under Kleisthenes' new constitution ten generals were appointed each year, one from each tribe. The first appointment of generals under the new system was not apparently carried out until 501, perhaps because Athens was still engaged in war with Sparta, Thebes, and then Chalkis at this time, or because the new tribal system took some years to become fully operational. Presumably during the period 508–501 the old system in which each of the four Ionic tribes appointed a general to command the tribe's hoplites continued.

The generals were nominated by each of the new tribal

37

assemblies (see p.27). It was acknowledged that the appointment of generals could not be left to selection by lot, and each tribe therefore put forward its most able candidate; a general, moreover, had to be at least 30 years old, which was a requirement for all magistrates. The final approval had to be given by the whole Assembly of citizens, but it seems they regularly accepted the nominations of the tribal assemblies. And in the case of generals there was no bar on repeated appointment year after year, and this certainly occurred, most notably in the case of Pericles, who was general for fifteen years in succession from 443 to 429.

The main task of the generals was to administer and command the Athenian armies and fleets, perhaps originally in tribal contingents, but the tribal responsibility seems quickly to have been superseded by a more collegiate responsibility. The generals had to be given a measure of autonomy in carrying out their responsibilities, especially when they were on active service away from Athens, but they were always accountable to the Assembly for their actions. Nevertheless, the role of general came to be one of the key power bases in the democracy, partly because Athens was almost permanently at war with somebody during the fifth century, but also because the position was the only formal state office filled on merit and which could be held for more than a year. Most of the prominent names in Athenian politics in the fifth century, from Miltiades and Themistocles, through Pericles to Nikias and Alkibiades were *strategoi*.

Under Kleisthenes' reforms, however, the ten *strategoi* were still under the command of the Polemarch, one of the nine arkhons, and this situation was still in force at the battle of Marathon in 490. The role of the Polemarch and the other arkhons was changed in 487/6, as we shall see later (p.52).

Some interesting figures are available for the appointment of generals. Before the Peloponnesian War (the figures come mainly from the period 441–431, but earlier more scattered figures seem to show the same pattern) about 60 per cent of generals came from the city demes and only 40 per cent from the coastal and inland demes put together. This presumably reflects the fact that it was much easier for those from the city demes to attend the tribal assemblies at which nominations for generals were made. But during the Peloponnesian War only 32 per cent come from the city demes, perhaps a result of the migration of population for many years of the war from the country areas into the area protected by the Long Walls (built between 461 and 458 to protect Athens and Peiraieus from land attack – see Map 2). At least people from the rural areas were more easily able to attend tribal assemblies.

The magistracies

The democracy needed administrators, and it needed quite a lot of them. The Athenians, however, did not employ a permanent civil service, but instead used the same principle of annual appointments from the citizen body as it used for the appointment of the *Boule*. We know that in the fourth century there were in total about 600 'magistrates' appointed each year. We have no precise figure for the fifth century, but it is likely that it was of the same order, doubtless increasing from a rather smaller number in Kleisthenes' time as the responsibilities of the state increased in areas such as public buildings, the navy and relations with the allies in the Delian League. Most magistrates operated in committees of ten, one from each tribe.

All magistrates had to be at least 30 thirty years old and had to come from the *pentakosiomedimnoi*, the *hippeis*, or the *zeugitai* classes; *thetes* were in theory excluded, but in practice they were gradually admitted. When in office they wore a wreath of myrtle leaves. In all these respects they were similar in status to members of the *Boule*, and like them they had to undergo a *dokimasia* (test) before taking up their appointment. In addition no person could hold a particular magistracy more than once in his lifetime, but there was no bar on holding different magistracies in different years, and we know of many people who held several over a period of years. In practice it was not possible to hold magistracies in consecutive years, since one had to undergo a clearing process known as *euthynai* (accounts; see p.41) after the year of office, and this was not completed until a few months after the term of office ended; until this was satisfactorily completed one could not hold another magistracy, so at least a year had to elapse between magistracies.

Some magistrates were elected and others were chosen by lot, though in both categories the general principle was that in the boards of ten there was one member from each tribe.

It seems about a hundred magistrates were elected (i.e. not

chosen by lot). These included the generals (who were strictly regarded as magistrates), the tribal regimental and cavalry commanders, those in charge of the training of the military conscripts (*epheboi*, all male citizens aged 18–20), the most important financial officers, and those comprising some boards in charge of religious matters. In all cases the justification for the election process rather than selection by lot was that a certain level of knowledge or expertise was required for the post. The election process took place at a special meeting of the Assembly about half-way through the year, around December since the Greek year started in mid-summer. This gave time for the *dokimasia* process to be properly carried out before those appointed took office. The full details of the election process are not known, but it seems one or more names were proposed from each tribe for each magistracy, and the Assembly voted for or against each person.

The other 500 magistrates were chosen by lot from those willing to stand. The different magistracies varied in status and popularity, but there was considerable competition for most, though we know some boards regularly operated with vacancies when a tribe provided no member. Tribes put forward their lists of names for each magistracy (with numbers varying from nil to several), and lots for each magistracy were then drawn, not in this case in the Assembly, since there was nothing to vote on, but in the Sanctuary of Theseus, which was located somewhere to the east of the Acropolis, presided over by the six arkhons who were *thesmothetai*. These magistracies (mostly in the usual boards of ten) included several concerned with control of markets, with weights and measures, and specifically with the corn supply; several boards to oversee various religious activities and festivals, including the upkeep of temples; a group of boards with various auditing functions to oversee the financial transactions of the state; and boards dealing with the maintenance of roads and with street cleaning, including control of dung collection and the removal of dead bodies from the streets. The Eleven have already been mentioned (see p.34); they were also appointed by lot, but why there were eleven and not ten we do not know. They were in charge of the state prison, dealt with property confiscated by the state, and had the power to carry out punishments, including execution, in cases where the accused (the *Athenaion Politeia* mentions specifically 'thieves, kidnappers and burglars') admitted their guilt, which looks like decidedly rough justice. There was in fact no state police force, though there was a squad of 300 Scythian archers (they were apparently genuine Scythians from south Russia) employed by the state from about 450, and they were at the disposal of certain boards of magistrates. We hear of them as keeping order at meetings of the Assembly, and before these meetings they apparently had the job of clearing the *agora* by dragging a red-painted rope around, though we are not sure whether this was a form of persuasion to attend the Assembly or for some other obscure purpose.

Submission of accounts (*euthynai*)

All magistrates were accountable during their term of office in the first instance to the *Boule* and through it to the Assembly. But also, as we have seen, at the end of their term of office all had to undergo the process of *euthynai* in which their conduct was scrutinised. This applied to all who held any public office, including the arkhons and the members of the Council of 500. A board of ten inspectors (*logistai*) organised this process soon after the beginning of each new administrative year, and its report on each board or individual magistrate was made to a special court of 501 members, at which any citizen could bring an accusation of malpractice, even if the *logistai* had made no complaint. The process was far from being a pure formality, and magistrates were very conscious of the need to keep their accounts straight and their actions within the law.

The magistrates were an essential part of the democratic system. All areas of public activity seem to have come under the responsibility of some magistrate or board of magistrates; if something was going wrong, people certainly knew who to blame.

The arkhons and the Council of
the Areopagos

Kleisthenes appears to have made virtually no formal change in the election or powers of the nine arkhons, except in so far as their election was now presumably carried out by the new Assembly, or in the powers of the Areopagos. The arkhons continued to be elected from the highest property class (the *pentakosiomedimnoi*, and perhaps also the *hippeis*), with no reference as far as we know to the tribal assemblies; the arkhons could therefore come from any of the new tribes.

Since under Solon's reforms the powers of the arkhons and of the Areopagos and the relationship of both to the Council of 400 and the shadowy assembly remain very indistinct, we can say little more than this. The arkhons' main role seems to have been in legal matters, and they continued to deal with all cases except those decided at deme level. It seems that the arkhons still carried out preliminary hearings when cases were first referred to them, as all cases were, but all citizens had the right of appeal to the new courts, just as they had had to Solon's *heliaia*, and this became an automatic process during the fifth century. It is possible that Ephialtes in 462/1 removed the powers of the arkhons to decide any case without referring it to the *dikasteria* (see p.54), but the real situation remains obscure. However, in general it seems safe to say that if the old Council of 400 was the overseer of all other magistrates from Solon's time, then the formal position of the arkhons was in no way changed when these responsibilities were taken over by the new *Boule*.

All arkhons continued to become members of the Areopagos at the end of their term of office, and the Areopagos was still the 'Guardian of the Laws', which, as we noted in considering Solon's reforms, must have given it considerable powers of veto, though we do not know how these operated. It remained the court for homicide cases. But the main powers of the Areopagos probably lay in the fact that it consisted of about 150 of the most wealthy and experienced men in Athens, and their opinions, both collectively and individually – and they doubtless let them be known forcefully in the Assembly – carried considerable weight. Moreover, being a member of the Areopagos was no bar to holding other office; Themistocles was arkhon in 493 and a *strategos* at Marathon in 490 and probably several times later.

Ostracism

Kleisthenes was very well aware of the potential danger of personal power and he devised a method by which the state could rid itself of any individual who was wielding too much influence. But the person concerned was not regarded as a criminal; he was banished from the state for ten years, but neither his property nor his status was in any way diminished. The system got the name 'ostracism' from the fact that the voting in this procedure was done on bits of broken pottery (*ostraka*, potsherds), the Greek equivalent of scrap paper. Around 11,000 *ostraka* inscribed with someone's name have survived from excavations in the *agora* and Kerameikos areas of Athens.

In the sixth prytany (in December) each year the Assembly was asked if it wished to carry out an ostracism that year. If it voted to do so, an ostracism was carried out in the following February or March. The procedure was that all those who wished to vote went by tribes into a specially constructed enclosure in the *agora* and there scratched the name of the person they wished to see removed from the state on a potsherd and cast this as their vote. The potsherds were then counted, and if there were at least 6,000 they were sorted by names and the person named on the largest number of potsherds was 'ostracised' and had to leave Attica within ten days and go into banishment for ten years. The procedure looks a little strange, but it did prevent a small group from forcing an ostracism and achieving their aim on a small turn-out on the day. Nevertheless, it is interesting to note that in the 1930s a heap of 191 *ostraka* was found in a well on the north slope of the Acropolis, all from pots of only a few different types and all inscribed with the name Themistocles written in only fourteen different hands. This was apparently a heap of pre-prepared *ostraka* made for distribution to voters who could be persuaded to vote against Themistocles. Since they were found all together, they are probably the left-overs from an originally bigger stock; the makers must have overestimated the popular opposition to Themistocles.

The first successful ostracism (of Hipparkhos, a relative of the tyrant Hippias) was carried out in 487. There were in total perhaps about a dozen ostracisms, the last (of the demagogue Hyperbolos) being in 417. The procedure was abandoned thereafter. (A full list of ostracisms is given in Appendix 2.)

Cleruchies and colonies

Klerukhiai (cleruchies) were a special kind of colony that the Athenians established in key locations around the Aegean. Though there is no evidence that they were a part of Kleisthenes' constitution, the system was first used to create a settlement on the island of Salamis only a year or two after Kleisthenes' reforms (a fragmentary inscription from the Acropolis, described in Meiggs and Lewis 1969, no. 14, records the event), and the regulations for cleruchies appear to have been devised as one of the early measures of the new democracy. In essence a cleruchy was a settlement of Athenian citizens set up in a strategically important location on an island or on the coast of the Aegean. In most cases (perhaps all) the land was taken from the local residents and, as Athens' Empire progressed, it was taken as a punitive measure after the revolt of an allied state. The settlers were called *klerukhoi* (cleruchs) from the fact that they were allocated a plot of land (*kleros*); a *klerukhos* simply means 'a person having an allotment'. Cleruchs were chosen mainly from the *thetes* class, the lowest property class, and they were given an allotment large enough to put them in the *zeugitai* class, the next higher group. The main cleruchies set up between 508 and 404 were Salamis (perhaps 507), Chalkis in Euboea (before 490), Lemnos and Imbros in the north Aegean (both around 480), Skyros in the west Aegean (about 475), Naxos and Andros in the south Aegean and the Chersonese (Gallipoli Peninsula) (all about 450), Hestiaia in Euboea (445), Aegina (431), and Lesbos (427) (see Map 1). A distinctive feature of the cleruchies appears to have been that settlers retained their full rights and duties as Athenian citizens, whereas other colonists became citizens of their new colony, though it must be said that this distinction may not be entirely correct. Colonies (not cleruchies) were also set up during this period, for example at Brea in Thrace (about 445; an inscription found in the Erechtheum on the Acropolis records the decision to set up the colony and details of how it is to be done; see Meiggs and Lewis 1969, no. 49), at Thurii in south Italy (443), and at Amphipolis in Thrace (437). Both types of settlement benefited the poorer classes in Athens by offering land, but they also created a network of Athenian strongholds.

State finance

We know of no specific financial measures introduced by Kleisthenes. In fact, his new constitution did not require any additional public expenditure, since it seems probable that there was no pay for any public office until about 460. However, it would be useful at this point to summarise the main features of the Athenian state economy, since financial considerations were a major part of the work of the various bodies of the democratic system and did inevitably play an important part in many political decisions. But it should be borne in mind that most of the information comes from the latter half of the fifth century, and we have no details at all from Kleisthenes' time.

State income came mainly from the ownership of property, in particular the silver mines at Laureion near Cape Sounion, from the 2 per cent tax (it may have been only 1 per cent in the fifth century) on all goods passing through the port of Peiraieus, and from fines and court fees. There was no income tax, though metics (foreigners resident in Athens) and prostitutes paid a form of poll tax. After the setting up of the Delian League there was an annual income from the allies to the League's treasury, initially of 460 talents but increasing to about 600 talents by the beginning of the Peloponnesian War. This income was, of course, ostensibly for the defence of the League, though this became increasingly a fiction; much was certainly spent on maintaining the fleet, but by 431 there was an accumulated surplus of 6,000 talents, though this was quickly dissipated in the first few years of the war. We know that the total internal income of Athens (i.e. excluding the income from the allies) just before the Peloponnesian War was about 400 talents, and this figure was probably not much greater than it had been in Kleisthenes' time, though we are admittedly guessing. It might be useful to convert this figure into something more tangible. In the late fifth century we know that a day's wage for a skilled labourer was one drachma a day, around 300 drachmas for a working year; and this figure is probably reasonably valid for the whole of the fifth century. There were 6,000 drachmas to the talent, so 400 talents is enough to pay 8,000 labourers for a year.

Other than the fleet, which was at least partly a charge against income from the allies, the main areas of expenditure for the state during the fifth century were as follows:

- defence, in the form of fortifications, the maintenance of the naval base near Peiraieus, and payment to soldiers when on active service;

- the organisation of religious festivals and the maintenance of temples;

- public works and buildings;

- after about 451/50, the payment of the members of the Boule and of magistrates and for attendance at the law courts.

The main variable amongst these was military expenditure. In times of all-out war the expenditure on pay for the armed forces was much increased, and ways had to be found to cover this; Athens' solution in 425 was to raise the tribute demanded from the allies to over 1,400 talents per year; the surplus of 6,000 talents had been eroded in six years!

But the organisation of the Athenian economy included a further essential feature, and this was the system known as *leitourgia*, usually but confusingly transcribed as 'liturgy'. The word means 'public work', which is an accurate description of what it was. In essence, rich men were expected to perform certain state tasks for one year at their own expense. When the system was introduced is unclear, but there is no reference to it before Kleisthenes and it seems well established by the early fifth century, so it may well have been introduced, at least in the form which is so well attested in the fifth century, as part of Kleisthenes' reforms.

The liturgies covered two areas of responsibility. The first category was the duty to contribute to the organisation and costs of running the numerous state religious ceremonies, and these included the great drama festivals where the liturgy was called the *choregia*, requiring rich patrons to train and equip the chorus for one of the plays. We know that in 472 Pericles was *choregos* for Aeschylus' 'Persians'. In all there were around a hundred of these *choregiai* to be carried out each year, some fairly modest but some quite expensive. The second category was known as the *trierarchia*, which involved the 'trierarch' in actually being captain of a trireme (though he always had a *kybernetes*, 'steersman', who was the experienced man in charge) and in maintaining it for a year, though the state paid for the building of the ships and for the crew. From the 480s onwards the Athenian fleet was never fewer than 200 triremes, so at least 200 trierarchs were required every year.

The liturgies were clearly a considerable burden, often costing a talent or more for the year. The same man could not be asked to perform a liturgy in two consecutive years, or two in the same year. During the Peloponnesian War the burden of *trierarchia* nevertheless became so great that the command of each trireme was shared between two men, each taking command for six months. The *trierarchia* was imposed only on citizens, but the festival liturgies were also allocated to wealthy metics. The allocation of festival liturgies was done by the arkhon, or by the tribe if the festival was organised by the tribe, and the *trierarchiai* were allocated by the generals. If anyone felt that there was someone else wealthier than himself who ought to carry out the liturgy allotted to him, then he could name the person and the person so challenged either had to take on the liturgy or agree to an exchange of property (*antidosis*) with the challenger. We do not in fact know of a single case where such an exchange was readily agreed, but we do know of several cases where a person challenged took the challenger to court, though in no case do we know the outcome. But despite the cost most rich people regarded the liturgies they had carried out (and many must have performed several) with pride, and vied with one another to provide things on a lavish scale. It is interesting to note that from what we know of the *leitourgia* system there must have been several hundred men each year (including metics) who could be called upon to find up to a talent (or occasionally even more) from their own resources to finance a liturgy.

The demes

All that we have dealt with so far in this chapter has been concerned with the government of the *state* as a corporate body. But we must not forget that the whole of the structure described above relied on an efficient organisation of each of the 139 demes. From numerous inscriptions found around Attica, and from literary references, we can get a fair picture of how the demes operated. (See Appendix 1 for a list of all demes.)

The demes were already regarded as organisational units long before Kleisthenes. In the rural areas (and we have to remember that the city of Athens itself was only a small part of the population of the otherwise rural Attica) a deme was essentially a village and its surrounding area, not necessarily clearly demarcated. In the city a deme was a sector with a name, reflecting, as in most cities, an earlier history when the various sectors were still fairly distinct village units. Kleisthenes made use of the demes as the basic unit of the new political system; each citizen had to be registered in the deme of which he considered himself a member, and thereafter he and his descendants normally remained members of that deme, even if they moved to another part of Attica. This explains why demes were not precise geographical units (at least not until the fourth century); they were essentially groupings of citizens who felt some allegiance to a particular deme, and they therefore consisted of a named place as the main focus, but with a scatter of people from rather further afield who regarded themselves as belonging to a particular deme because of family or other reasons.

Each deme had a *demarkhos* (demarch), the political head of the deme, and this office was actually instituted by Kleisthenes. The demarch was chosen annually, perhaps originally by vote but later (perhaps from 451/0) by lot. The larger demes had several other officers, mainly treasurers and religious officials, but the smaller demes apparently made do with just the demarch. Each deme had an Assembly of all its citizens, with the demarch as president. This Assembly must have met at least once a year, and in larger demes probably several times a year.

The main business of the demarch, and ultimately of the Deme Assembly, can be summarised as follows:

- Maintaining an accurate record of all citizens in the deme. This was an essential task, since registration as a member of a deme was in effect registration as a citizen of Athens. It was the duty of the deme to check on the validity of each citizen's registration.

- Carrying out various duties concerning local cults, including the care of temples, the celebration of festivals, offering sacrifices, and the collection of rents on sacred lands.

- Acting as an agent for the state, for example in organising the levying of naval forces (though they were organised by tribe when on active service, it was the demes which actually decided who should be chosen to serve at any particular time), performing certain religious rites on behalf of the state, and collecting certain taxes imposed from time to time by the state.

- Selecting each year the deme's quota of members for the *Boule* (the Council of 500). We do not know exactly how this was done, but there does seem to have been at least an element of selection by lot even at deme level, perhaps amongst those willing to stand if there were more of them than the deme's allocation of *Boule* members; though there may have been selection by lot from all who were eligible.

- Approving inscriptions in honour of eminent citizens of the deme, especially of those who had paid for the numerous religious festivals. From the number of inscriptions which survive, it seems that this was an important part of the work of the Deme Assembly.

As in all the institutions of the democracy, the officers were responsible to the citizen body, and the Deme Assembly each year carried out the process of *euthynai* (accounts) on the out-going officers of the deme.

Democracy at deme level was an important feature of Athenian life, and an excellent training ground for the democratic institutions at state level. Democracy did indeed permeate Athenian life.

Why did Kleisthenes do it?

Kleisthenes' name will forever be associated with the invention of Athenian democracy. Though Solon's reforms had produced a version of democracy, and had in particular created a judicial system which was essentially in the hands of the citizen body, the tyranny of the Peisistratids had decidedly blunted its edge, and Kleisthenes' reforms went far further in putting the state in the corporate power of the citizens. And yet the Alkmeonid family which Kleisthenes headed had hardly been well known for democratic ideals, and some later members of the family seemed less than enthusiastic for democracy. One must ask how far Kleisthenes was aware of the likely consequences of his reforms.

Kleisthenes was undoubtedly under great pressure from his non-aristocratic supporters, after his return from exile in 508, to prevent the constant warring amongst the aristocratic families. We know nothing of what negotiations took place, but one suspects that there was a lot of hard bargaining and compromise, forgotten later because the democracy worked and had Kleisthenes' name attached to it. It is worth noting that Kleisthenes left the arkhons in a position of considerable power, and the Areopagos, being a council of ex-arkhons, remained a body with great prestige, even though this situation lasted only some twenty years after Kleisthenes' reforms. Perhaps he saw the arkhons as an essential foil to the new powers of the *Boule* and the Assembly. We have seen in some detail the ten-tribe system that was set up, and there is no doubt that this system did indeed very effectively hinder any aristocratic family from dominating Athens from then on as long as the democracy lasted. Kleisthenes may well have tried to retain some kind of power base within the new structure for his own family, as we have seen (pp.25–7), by judicious manipulation of the *trittyes* in his home territories to the south of Athens and perhaps in those on the east coast, but if he hoped for any real advantage to accrue to the Alkmeonids from this then he and they were to be disappointed, because quite simply this manoeuvring was just not enough to secure much real control. The new systems worked all too well, and the power of the arkhons was soon to be seen as an anomaly. The leaders who emerged in the democracy gained their positions, not from the support of aristocratic families and retainers (which some did indeed have), but from their ability to persuade the demes, the tribal assemblies, the *Boule*, and the Assembly, and this is just as true of Pericles, who married into the Alkmeonid family, as of anyone else.

On the other hand Kleisthenes may have been convinced of the rightness of a radical democracy and had the vision to devise a structure which would develop its own momentum and allow the citizen body to decide its own future. This is the reputation which, for the most part, he has enjoyed. We may perhaps be justified in wondering if this is quite the way he looked at it.

this must also have been in the minds of those who proposed the change. Since the average age of entry into the Areopagos is likely to have been around 40 to 50, it would not take long for the change to selection by lot to alter the make-up of the Areopagos, and with it the status and respect it had previously enjoyed. After ten years probably about half its members were from those selected by lot, and after twenty years only a small minority can have been left of those who had been elected on merit (or, perhaps more accurately, of those favoured by the wealthier property classes and approved by the Assembly). This time-scale is significant.

In 462/1 Ephialtes, a firm democrat about whom we know all too little, proposed to the Assembly that the Areopagos should be stripped of most of its powers, arguing that many of its powers were 'acquired'. The timing of his proposal to the Assembly was well planned. In 462 Kimon, pursuing his pro-Spartan policy, had got the Assembly to agree to send him and 4,000 hoplites to the Peloponnese to help Sparta to suppress a slave revolt (unsuccessfully as it turned out; see pp.61–2). In the absence of 4,000 of the wealthier citizens who might well have opposed the measure, Ephialtes' proposal was accepted by the Assembly. We do not know exactly what Ephialtes meant by 'acquired', but presumably it implies that the Areopagos had acquired powers (we do not know what these were) which were not formally included in Solon's or in Kleisthenes' reforms; in fact one suspects that the constitutional powers of the Areopagos had never been formally defined either by Solon or by Kleisthenes. One power it certainly had had since Solon's time was as 'Guardian of the Laws', which probably gave the Areopagos the power to intervene and to apply a veto if the Council of 500 or the Assembly or any magistrate acted or proposed to act 'unconstitutionally'. We have no evidence to indicate how this worked in practice, but it must have been the basis of the Areopagos' continuing influence, and it may have been an excessive use of this power to intervene in the workings of the democracy that Ephialtes was complaining about. Whatever the details, in 462/1 Ephialtes passed a measure to limit the powers of the Areopagos, in effect stripping it of all its controlling and supervisory powers and leaving it only as a court for cases of homicide and certain offences of sacrilege. In his *Eumenides*, performed in 458, Aeschylus goes to some lengths to portray the

53

Areopagos as a most dignified court established by Athena herself, initially to try Orestes but then to continue in perpetuity as the homicide court for Athens. In the play Athena herself appears and sets up the Court of the Areopagos:

Athena People of Athens! As you now begin to judge this first case of bloodshed, hear the constitution of this court. From this day forward this judicial council shall for Aigeus' race try every such case. Here shall be its perpetual seat, on Ares' Hill.

(Aeschylus, *Eumenides* 681–5)

Though the play is certainly not a political pamphlet, one has the impression that Aeschylus, himself from a noble family, is trying to preserve the dignity of a severely battered institution. But its political powers were now gone. The introduction of selection of the nine arkhons by lot in 487/6 had altered the range and probably the calibre of new members. It seems that even at the time of Xerxes' invasion in 480 the Areopagos still retained considerable prestige, while the majority of its members had still been appointed arkhon by direct election. But the post-Salamis generation, confident in their triremes, which were manned by thousands of ordinary citizens, controlling now a new Aegean empire, saw the Areopagos with its increasing number of members selected by lot as an anomaly in the patently successful democracy. Ephialtes' reform of the Areopagos doubtless seemed to many a natural development. Soon after Ephialtes' reforms, or maybe as part of them, the arkhonship and hence the Areopagos was made open to the *zeugitai* class as well as to the two higher property classes; the Areopagos had been democratised. It may also have been at this time that the power of the arkhons to try cases themselves without referring them to the *dikasteria* was removed. The automatic referral of all cases to the *dikasteria* appears to have become the normal practice about this time, and such a move does seem to fit in well with Ephialtes' reforms.

The *graphe paranomon*

But now that the Areopagos was no longer 'Guardian of the Laws', who was responsible for ensuring that the constitution was preserved? The problem was resolved by the introduction of the *graphe paranomon* (prosecution for introducing illegal measures). This enabled any citizen to bring an action (a *graphe*, a public prosecution) against any other citizen who proposed a measure in the Assembly which was either in conflict with existing law (other than measures which were overtly amendments to existing laws) or which was procedurally incorrect. The case was then tried by a court, usually, as for any *graphe* trial, with a jury panel of 501 (see pp.34–7, for procedures). If the offending proposal had not yet been agreed by the Assembly, the proposal was held in abeyance until the court made its decision; if the proposal had already been approved by the Assembly (and this did happen), the court could annul the decision of the Assembly. In either case, if the person bringing the *graphe paranomon* won his case, he would receive a reward and the mover of the unconstitutional proposal would be fined – though, as in all *graphe* trials, the person bringing the action risked a fine of 1,000 drachmas and loss of civic rights if he did not get at least a fifth of the votes of the court. This system was certainly more democratic than having the Areopagos as the constitutional watchdog, though one might question its efficiency and its objectivity.

It would seem logical for Ephialtes to have introduced the *graphe paranomon* at the same time as he removed from the Areopagos its role as 'Guardian of the Laws'. In fact, the first recorded use of the *graphe paranomon* is from 415 or a little before, some forty-five years after Ephialtes' reforms. This could indicate that the issue was simply not seen as a problem for some years after Ephialtes' reforms and that the *graphe paranomon* was introduced perhaps in the Peloponnesian War when problems of constitutional precedent may have become more acute. But our records of the fifth century BC are far from full, and it is unwise to argue from silence. The removal from the Areopagos of its role as 'Guardian of the Laws' was apparently a major issue (this and the associated legislation was probably the main reason for Ephialtes' assassination, which occurred soon after 462/1), and it seems unlikely that Ephialtes did not take measures at the time to fill this constitutional gap. It is probably better to assume that we simply do not happen to have any record of the use of the *graphe paranomon* until well into the Peloponnesian War.

Ephialtes remains a shadowy figure, and we do not possess a coherent account of his reforms in 462/1. In terms of the logic of constitutional reform it looks as if the reforms of the Areopagos and the introduction of the *graphe paranomon* were all part of one package, but it has to be admitted that it may not really have been quite so tidy. A point worthy of note is that Pericles, in his early 30s at the time of Ephialtes' reforms, worked closely with Ephialtes in carrying through these reforms.

Introduction of 'deme-judges'

Peisistratos had introduced 'deme-judges' to deal with minor disputes at local level, but we hear nothing of such people again until 453/2, when the idea seems to have been revived. Thirty deme-judges were now appointed. We have no further information at all, but the number makes it look as if there was one appointed for each *trittys*. Presumably they acted as the first layer of the justice system; cases could if necessary go forward to the relevant arkhon, and then on to the courts in Athens.

Payment for dikasts, magistrates and members of the *Boule*

Kleisthenes' reform of the law courts, as we have seen, required 6,000 citizens each year to be registered as dikasts. But the commitment in acting as a dikast was considerable; for those who took the task seriously and came early in the day for selection to their allotted court, there were potentially 200 days of court sessions each year. Of course, dikasts could simply not turn up if they had more pressing commitments, but the system clearly favoured those who could afford not to work on court days. A few years after Ephialtes' reforms, probably around 451/50, Pericles introduced payment for dikasts. The pay was two obols a day (there were six obols to a drachma), or at least it was in the early years of the Peloponnesian War when it was increased from two to three obols, and two obols was probably the rate fixed in 451/50. This was a bare subsistence rate for one person. One could certainly not keep a family on it, but it was an attempt to encourage even the poorest citizens to offer themselves as dikasts; and it does seem to have had the desired effect.

It seems that about the same time, or perhaps a little later, payment was also introduced for magistrates and members of the *Boule*. They probably received the same daily rate as dikasts, though we do not have details for this period.

Citizenship

It was also in 451/50 that Pericles carried a law that in future citizenship would be confined to those whose parents were *both* Athenian; previously to have an Athenian father was sufficient to confirm citizenship. The effect of this was, of course, to reduce the citizen numbers in future, though probably not greatly, and the measure seems to have had more to do with Pericles' efforts to court popularity. It did have the effect of making the rights and privileges of citizenship somewhat more exclusive, and though this measure undoubtedly alienated a few it gained the support of the large majority of citizens who saw themselves as members of a more exclusive club. Clever politics – but it rebounded later on Pericles in a very personal way. Around 445 he divorced his wife and lived with Aspasia, a woman from Miletos in Ionia. They had a son, also called Pericles, who was not of course an Athenian citizen. In fact, after Pericles' death in the plague in 429, the younger Pericles was granted citizenship. He was one of the ill-fated generals at the naval battle of Arginoussai (near the island of Lesbos) in 406, and was executed after the battle with his surviving fellow generals.

We noted above that all these changes during the fifth century were in the direction of greater participation by the citizen body. We might also note that Pericles probably had a hand in them all, first in association with Ephialtes, and then as the leading democrat in Athens.

Legislation

In the field of law-making a procedural change took place after the Peloponnesian War. Since Kleisthenes' time new laws had been made by proposals being put to the Assembly, which decided by a simple majority whether or not the proposal should become law. In 410, when democracy had been restored after the oligarchic revolution of 411, a full codification of the law was begun. A specially appointed board of *nomothetai* ('lawsetters'; the word means almost the same as *thesmothetai*, but a different title was needed for the new board) was set up to carry out the task. It was a major undertaking; in essence it involved compiling a full list of the laws of Drakon and Solon (still at the end of the fifth century the main sources of private law) together with all the laws passed by the Assembly since Kleisthenes' reforms, which themselves must also have been part of this codification. The task was not finally completed until 400/399. After the full codification was published a new procedure was introduced in which all legislative proposals, after prēliminary discussion by the *Boule* and by the Assembly, were put to a board of *nomothetai* (the same title was used for a new board in what now became a regular procedure), chosen by lot from the 6,000 men who were registered each year as dikasts and had taken the 'Heliastic Oath' (see p.36). The procedure with the *nomothetai* worked in effect as a court, with speeches made for and against the proposed new laws. The board of *nomothetai* then voted on each new proposal, and their decision was final. This may appear at first sight as a diminution of the powers of the Assembly, but in practice it was not so, since the Assembly still decided whether or not proposals should go to the *nomothetai*. The procedure removed a lot of tedious and often technical business from the Assembly, whose agendas were crowded enough.

5

The system in practice

So how did the system actually work in practice? The democratic system did of course permeate the social and political life
of Athens; there was little that Athenians did, or even thought,
that was not in some way affected by the remarkable democratic
system which they had developed from 508 onwards. In order
to see how the democratic institutions actually functioned, and
to get a feel of what Athenians themselves thought about them,
in this chapter we shall follow through four themes, each with
a very different perspective but all focusing on how Athenians
used their democratic system. We shall begin with a survey of
the key political decisions of the period from Marathon to just
after 450, the period which saw Athens reach the height of its
influence through the development of its fleet and the estab-
lishment of the Delian League, which quickly became an Athenian Empire. Then we shall follow in outline the career of
Pericles, in particular identifying how he managed to control so
effectively the policies of the now elaborate democracy. Thirdly
we shall look at some of the views expressed by the comedy
playwrights, concentrating necessarily on Aristophanes since
many of his plays survive whereas we have only fragments
(though very interesting fragments) of the others. And finally we
shall hear from 'The Old Oligarch'; we do not know who he
was, but he had little time for the cumbersome procedures of
the democracy or for the 'worthless people' who dominated it.

We have already seen some of the key developments of the Athenian democracy which took place during and to some extent because of the Persian Wars. At Marathon the role of the Polemarch was clearly seen to be redundant now that there were ten generals elected by their tribes for their military capability. In 487/6 the Assembly decided that arkhons should in future be chosen by lot from 500 candidates. But it was Themistocles' insistence on the development of a strong Athenian fleet with the income from the rich seams discovered in the Laureion silver mines in 483 that really put the *demos* into a position of power. Themistocles' immediate aim was of course to build a fleet that could withstand another Persian invasion, and the fact that Aegina had a bigger fleet than Athens at the time was a strong incentive for the Assembly to vote for the newly discovered wealth to be spent on a fleet rather than to be distributed equally amongst Athenian citizens. But it is interesting to note that Aristeides, one of the generals at Marathon with Miltiades and Themistocles, arkhon in 489/8 and well known for his more conservative views, opposed Themistocles' policy – and was ostracised in 482 probably as a direct result. Aristeides and others from the wealthier end of the social spectrum doubtless saw (as Themistocles must have done too) that the consequence of putting so much of the state's available resources into the fleet would be that those who manned the fleet (almost entirely poorer citizens from the *thetes* class, mostly labourers with little or no land of their own) would see themselves as the main armed forces of the state, which they certainly became. The hoplites, who were recruited entirely from the wealthier citizens, mainly landowners, who could buy their own arms, and who had gained such a reputation at Marathon, would be much reduced in importance.

Salamis completely justified Themistocles' policy. Without their much enlarged fleet the Athenians could not possibly have defeated the Persians. And Aristeides was exactly right; Salamis was a tremendous boost for the morale of the Athenian poorer classes. It was they who manned the fleet which defeated Xerxes, and it was they who in effect controlled the Assembly. In Xerxes' invasion the role of the Athenian hoplites was much less significant. But Aristeides' own career warns us against any simple view of party struggle in Athenian politics. In 480 he was recalled from exile in the general amnesty occasioned by Xerxes' invasion and worked closely with Themistocles. In the battle of Salamis, as one of the ten generals, he headed the hoplites who landed on the island of Psyttaleia. In 479 he commanded the Athenian hoplites at the battle of Plataea, under the overall command of the Spartan Pausanias. In 478 he was commander of the Athenian fleet in the Aegean and won over parts of the Ionian coast from Pausanias. In 477 he gained a great reputation for his organisation of the tribute allocations in the formation of the Delian League. Aristeides ('the Just' was his nickname) was from the old aristocracy, and he resisted the move to a more radical democracy. But when it came he played a full part in it. Unlike many from the old noble families, he was not pro-Spartan, and he seems to have seen the Delian League as a legitimate expression of Athenian power – the sea power which he had himself opposed in 483.

After the defeat of the Persians Themistocles' influence quickly waned. We do not know the exact reason; the historian Plutarch says simply that the Athenian *demos* had had enough of him. (Plutarch, Kimon, 5). Aristeides, as we have seen, returned to prominence, but the dominant figure of the twenty years or so after Salamis was Kimon, son of the hero of Marathon, Miltiades. But not only was he the son of a famous father (though Miltiades himself was fined fifty talents after his failure to capture the island of Paros in 489 and died soon after of his wounds); he also allied himself with the Alkmeonid family by marrying Isodike, grand-niece of Kleisthenes, around 480. From 478 to 463 Kimon commanded most of the naval operations in the Aegean, being general of his tribe for all or most of this period. About 471 Themistocles was ostracised, partly because he was involved in some way with Pausanias' various misdeeds in Ionia, but partly because Kimon still saw him as a rival. After various adventures Themistocles ended his days as governor of a Persian province.

Kimon pursued a policy of friendship with Sparta. In 462 Sparta appealed to Athens for help in suppressing a revolt of the Helot slave population, and when this appeal was put before the Assembly Kimon strongly supported the Spartan request. He was opposed by Ephialtes, who saw no point at all in risking Athenian forces to help Sparta. But such was Kimon's popularity that the Assembly voted for a force of 4,000 hoplites under Kimon's command to go to help the Spartans to crush the Helot revolt. But things did not go well. The combined forces of Sparta and her various allies could not capture the Helot stronghold of Ithome in Messenia, and Kimon and his hoplites were simply asked to leave. It was while Kimon and the 4,000 hoplites were away from home that Ephialtes (with Pericles as his collaborator) carried out his radical reform of the Areopagos (see pp.53–4). Under the influence of Ephialtes the Assembly had swung very decisively in the direction of radical democracy, so much so that Kimon, whose rejection by Sparta had in any case destroyed his pro-Spartan policy, was ostracised in 461. On his return from exile in 451 he did in fact play a major role in the peace treaty with Sparta which was concluded that year, but the following year he died on campaign in Cyprus. Kimon may well have had the support of members of the Alkmeonid family; but it is very clear that by this time the Alkmeonids were not a united political faction – Pericles' mother Agariste was the niece of Kleisthenes.

Themistocles, Aristeides, Kimon and then Pericles all contri-buted to the development of the Delian League, which soon became (some would argue it always was) an Athenian Empire, in the sense that Athens controlled it completely. They operated through the Assembly and its various administrative bodies, all of them as generals of their tribes. The generals were, as we have seen, the only officers of the state who could be re-appointed year after year. The Assembly, most of whose members had at some time rowed in a trireme, was happy to be persuaded by these capable generals to use Athens' naval superiority to create an empire; the Assembly never questioned its own right to expand and control this empire. It brought employment, on the triremes, on the docks, in trade, it brought prosperity, partly through trade with the allies in the League and partly because the grain supply from the Black Sea was now protected by the fleet, and it brought a real sense of power to every citizen. After Ephialtes' reforms of 462/1 that power lay solely and exclusively in the hands of the members of the Assembly, and they in-creasingly resented any interference, either from Sparta or from their own allies. A few key decisions well illustrate this in-exorable imperialism:

- Naxos (in 469/8) and Thasos (in 465), both large islands contributing ships in Aristeides' scheme of 477, wished to withdraw from the Delian League. The response of the Assembly was the same in both cases: both were blockaded and forced to continue as tribute-paying members of the League.

- In 454 the treasury of the League was moved from Delos to Athens, and each city in the League now had to bring its tribute to Athens. From this time Tribute Lists recording the payments to the goddess Athena, which were one-sixtieth of each city's tribute, were carved in stone and displayed on the Acropolis. Substantial fragments of these lists have been found.

- Immediately after the Peace of Kallias (449) there is a complete year missing in the Tribute Lists, and the following year shows many partial payments or non-payments of tribute. The likely interpretation of this is that the allies saw no point now in paying to be defended against Persia. The response of the Assembly is contained in a decree of which sections still survive. The mover is Kleinias, an associate of Pericles:

> The *Boule* and the *Demos* [i.e. the Assembly] have decided . . . that the *Boule*, the governors in the cities [i.e. Athenian officials based in the allied cities] and the inspectors [more Athenian officials!] shall see to it that the tribute payments be collected each year and be brought to Athens . . . and let the *prytaneis* summon the Assembly for the *Hellenotamiai* [the Athenian treasures of the League] to make known to the Athenians which of the cities have paid the tribute money in full and which have fallen short . . .
>
> (Meiggs and Lewis 1969, no. 46)

The Assembly is clearly taking a hard line against those allies who think that now peace has been made with Persia their city can stop its payments to Athens. The opening formula ('The *Boule* and the *Demos* have decided . . .') is the regular one for decrees of the Assembly, and illustrates the normal procedure in which the *Boule* brings proposals to the Assembly; if the Assembly agrees, the decree specifies that both the *Boule* and the Assembly have made the decision. This decree also makes it clear that the *Boule* has the administrative task, together with the appropriate magistrates, of carrying out the decree.

Athens of course favoured democratic governments among its allies, though it did tolerate other kinds of government if they were compliant to Athenian demands. But we have a clear example of Athens imposing a democratic constitution on a member of the Delian League in the 'Erythrai Decree'. This was in the form of an inscription on stone found on the Acropolis, though the original has now been lost. Erythrai was a small city on the Ionian coast opposite the island of Chios. The city did not pay tribute in 453/2, probably because it had revolted against Athenian control, but in 450/449 it paid *twice*. The Erythrai Decree is apparently the settlement which Athens imposed on Erythrai after it had been brought back into line, probably in 451. The Decree is thirty-seven lines long and makes quite detailed arrangements for setting up a new government. The details for the new Council are as follows:

> The Council shall consist of 120 men, chosen by lot . . . and no alien shall be a member of the Council nor anyone less than thirty years of age. . . . No-one shall serve on the Council twice within four years . . .
>
> The Council shall swear as follows: 'I will take such counsel, as far as I am able, as shall be best and most just for the people of Erythrai and of Athens and of their allies; and I will not revolt from the people of Athens . . .'
>
> (Meiggs and Lewis 1969, no. 40)

The size and appointment arrangements for the Council are obviously based on the Athenian Council of 500, but reflect the needs of a much smaller city state. And the councillors' oath makes it very clear that by now the Delian League was not a voluntary defence federation against Persia!

The Athenian Empire was definitely a good thing in the eyes of the Assembly in Athens. All they needed was capable generals and political leaders (usually the same people) of a like mind. From about 460 until his death in 429 they certainly had one in Pericles.

Pericles

Many volumes have been written about Pericles. Here we shall concentrate briefly on the way he operated within the democratic system. Pericles has already been mentioned several times in the preceding pages, but it is useful to bring together the evidence for the way he acted within the democratic structures in order to understand Pericles himself and also the operation of the democracy. Pericles was by any standards a great leader, and he is all the more intriguing because he was not a king or a dictator or even an elected head of state, but a member (one hesitates to say an ordinary member) of a radical democracy one of whose principles was that all powers were held corporately and within which all officers of the state were annually account-able to the Council of 500 and ultimately to the Assembly.

Pericles' mother Agariste was the niece of Kleisthenes. His father Xanthippos commanded the Athenian contingent of the fleet at the battle of Mykale in 479, the last battle of the Persian Wars. Before that, as an ally of the Alkmeonids though not himself a member of the family, he had led the prosecution of Miltiades in 489, then he had been ostracised in 485/4, quite probably because of his links with the Alkmeonids (he was married to Agariste by now), whose leader Megacles had been ostracised in 486, just a year after Hipparkhos, the last promin-ent Peisistratid, had also been ostracised. It looks as if there was strong opposition to the Alkmeonids at this time, perhaps because of suspicion that they were in contact with the Persians – and maybe still with Hippias, a suspicion which incidentally lends support to the view that Kleisthenes (head of the family before Megacles) may not have been as dedicated to the ideals of democracy as tradition has made him out to be. Xanthippos, it seems, shared in this unpopularity of the Alkmeonids, but he returned to Athens under the amnesty at the time of Xerxes' invasion in 480 and certainly redeemed himself in the eyes of the Athenian *demos* not only by his command of the Athenian fleet at Mykale, but also by his success in 478 in taking Sestos (on the Hellespont), after the Spartans had lost interest in any further action against Persia and had gone home, and by executing the Persian governor and his children.

Pericles was born about 495. His father died some time before 463, but Pericles certainly inherited his father's opposition to Persia, and also his independence of Sparta. His first political action was to contribute to the prosecution of Kimon in 463 which resulted from criticism of his accounts (*euthynai*) after his campaigns as a general to subdue the island of Thasos, which had revolted from the League. As we have noted, Kimon's wife and Pericles' mother were both descendants of Kleisthenes, but politically they were far apart. Whilst Kimon supported close links with Sparta, Pericles most certainly did not. In fact, in the trial on his *euthynai* Kimon was acquitted.

The sequence of events in the next two years, 462 and 461, is unfortunately not entirely clear, but the following reconstruction seems likely. Pericles, now in his early 30s, had joined Ephialtes, but still very much as the junior partner, and they had carried out several political attacks on members of the Areopagos. It was in the summer of 462, as we have already seen (pp.61–2), that Kimon persuaded the Assembly, much against the advice of Ephialtes, to send him as general with 4,000 hoplites to help the Spartans to suppress the revolt of their Helot slaves. They must have been gone at least a few months, enough time for Ephialtes finally to push through his reforms of the Areopagos (see pp.53–4). When Kimon returned to Athens his pro-Spartan policy was discredited, and in the spring of 461 he was ostracised. But very soon after that Ephialtes was dead, murdered by a hired killer, and Pericles found himself the leading radical democrat, with Kimon away in exile.

Pericles' dominance in Athenian politics from this time until his death in 429 was due to his consistent policy of developing and asserting Athenian naval supremacy, which he realised and accepted would always create conflict with Sparta and its allies, and to his ability to express his proposals in a compelling way in the Assembly. In fact he did not speak frequently in the Assembly, but when he did he made sure the issue was a major one and his views were absolutely clear. He undoubtedly caught the prevailing mood of the *demos*, who saw real benefits in his expansionist policies. His policies provided employment for large numbers of citizens in the triremes and in trades associated with the navy, and also provided the income from the members of the Delian League to pay for all this; it was in fact a sophisticated protection racket. The League also provided a kind of common market for its members, though Athens probably benefited most, partly because of the 2 per cent tax collected on all imports and exports at Peiraieus, and partly because it was the biggest industrial centre in Greece and had goods and skills to sell. It is little wonder that Pericles' action in 451/50 to restrict the citizenship in future to those whose parents were both citizens was a popular move, since by then the advantages of being an Athenian citizen and the feeling of power it gave were very real.

Pericles strongly favoured the setting up of cleruchies, and it was on his instigation that cleruchs were sent to Naxos, Andros, Thrace and the Chersonese (all about 450–45). The colonies at Thurii in south Italy (443), Amphipolis (437), and possibly the earlier one at Brea in Thrace (about 445) were also set up under his instigation. This sudden increase in colonisation fits well with Pericles' policies of Athenian naval supremacy and attractive deals for the *demos*. It may also indicate that the citizenship law of 451/50 did have something to do with rising numbers in the citizen population, since these settlements together took around 4,000 citizens out of Athens.

It was Pericles who in 448 initiated the policy of using income from the Delian League to rebuild the temples on the Acropolis that had been destroyed in the Persian invasions. He did try to organise a pan-Hellenic conference with this proposal on the agenda, doubtless as a way of gaining moral support from states outside the League for a proposal he knew would be unpopular within it. But the conference never met, and he went ahead anyway. With the Assembly, of course, the building project was immensely popular. It glorified Athens, it confirmed Athens as the leading city in Greece, and it provided employment. But there was opposition. Thucydides son of Melesias (he is usually so called to distinguish him from the historian Thucydides, though they were related) was now the leader of the aristocratic opposition to Pericles. He was related by marriage to Kimon, and after Kimon's death in 450 he had become the leader of the aristocratic families, whose wealth still came mainly from land and who saw little for them in Pericles' imperial policies; indeed there *was* little for them in the expansion of Athenian power in the Aegean. But the line Thucydides took in opposing Pericles' building policy was a moral one, that this was an unjust use of the money contributed by the allies for defence against Persia. Pericles argued that the allies were paying for defence and they were getting it; what else Athens did with the money it received was entirely up to Athens. In 443 Pericles proposed that the issue should be tested by an ostracism. He must have been confident that he himself was in little danger of exile, and he was right; Thucydides was ostracised. Thucydides' departure removed the last organised opposition to Pericles.

Pericles had been several times general of his tribe before 443, often on military expeditions around the Aegean, but from 443 he was general of his tribe every year until his death in 429, with the exception of a short period which will be discussed below. This did in fact create something of a problem, in that if the rule of one general from each tribe each year were strictly adhered to that meant that any other able candidate from Pericles' tribe (he was from the city deme of Cholargos in the tribe of Akamantis) would be excluded from being general. However, we know that in several years (441, 439, 433, 432 and perhaps 431) *two* generals were appointed from the Akamantis tribe (Pericles and one other), and one of the other tribes had no general. This probably required no formal legislation, since it was the Assembly which finally appointed the ten generals from the nominations of the tribes, and presumably the Akamantis tribe made their case for two generals, perhaps in collaboration with another tribe who agreed not to make a nomination. Since by this time the generals do not appear to have commanded their tribal contingents in person, this arrangement was quite workable.

In 430, a year after the outbreak of the Peloponnesian War, the Athenians were huddled inside the Long Walls because of the Spartan invasion of Attica, and the plague hit Athens. Pericles had indeed planned that the population of Attica would shelter within the Long Walls, crowded though it was, but he had not bargained for the plague. His popularity quickly waned as the plague devastated the Athenian population, and in the summer of 430 he was not elected general of his tribe and he was also fined (fifteen talents or fifty, accounts vary; it was anyhow a lot of money) for maladministration in the *euthynai* process. But by the following spring it became evident that the generals who had been elected were not dealing with the situation, and Pericles was therefore somehow (the process is unclear) elected general in mid-term. But in the autumn of 429 Pericles himself died of the plague.

Aristophanes and the comedians

It is unfortunate that we have only fragments of two of the three great comedy writers of the fifth century, since in antiquity Cratinos and Eupolis were put on a par with Aristophanes, the only one of the three whose work still survives in any quantity.

These three dominated what is usually termed 'Old Comedy', which is the comic theatre of the latter half of the fifth century in Athens. The loss of the works of Cratinos and Eupolis is not only literary but also historical, since one of the features of Old Comedy was its open criticism of the policies and politicians of the day.

Cratinos was the oldest of the three, and he seems to have begun writing comic plays from at the latest about 450. From a play which must have been performed soon after the ostracism of Thucydides in 443 we have the following fragment:

> Here comes Pericles, our onion-headed Zeus, with a hat the size of the Concert Hall on his head, now that we've held the ostracism.
>
> (Cratinos, Fragment in *Oxford Book of Greek Verse*, 298)

Pericles had a strangely shaped head (Cratinos strictly says 'like a squill', which is a kind of onion) which bulged at the back. He seems to have been very self-conscious about this, and statues portray him with a helmet tipped backwards to conceal his bump. 'Zeus', of course, refers to his almost kingly status in Athens. The reference to the hat, strictly 'the size of the Odeion', the great concert hall near the Acropolis, on the east side of the Theatre of Dionysos, which had a large tent-like roof and had just been built as part of Pericles' building programme, is doubtless intended to remind the audience of Pericles' habit of wearing big hats to hide his odd-shaped head, and also of the controversial architecture of Pericles' new building. And Pericles is apparently strutting about proudly now he has got Thucydides ostracised.

Eupolis was more or less contemporary with Aristophanes, and like Aristophanes he began writing early, probably in his late teens. The following fragment praising Pericles' ability as an orator in the Assembly cannot be dated accurately, but is certainly some years after Pericles' death and is probably meant as a contrast with the poorer speakers of his own day:

> He surpassed all other men as a speaker. Whenever he came to the front to speak, he was like a top-class runner, giving the others a ten-foot start but then overtaking them all. He spoke quickly, but along with the speed there was persuasion on his lips. This was how he charmed you, and he was the

only speaker who used to leave his sting embedded in the audience.

(Eupolis, Fragment in *Oxford Book of Greek Verse*, 440)

Many other writers make the point that one of Pericles' great talents was his ability to persuade an audience of 5,000 or more in the Assembly.

Aristophanes (*c*.450–385) wrote about forty comedies of which eleven survive complete, and we have fragments from many of the others. The earliest of his surviving plays is the *Acharnians*, produced in January/February 425. All but two (the *Assemblywomen* from 392 and *Wealth* from 382) of the surviving plays come from the period of the Peloponnesian War. Aristophanes frequently portrays the democracy at work, often satirising the democratic institutions and the way they worked. His attitude is essentially conservative. He is not against the democracy, but he is against those who mislead the Assembly for their own ends.

The *Acharnians* opens with Dikaiopolis, an old farmer, sitting alone in the Pnyx waiting for a meeting of the Assembly (a Main Meeting, an *ekklesia kyria*) to begin. So far he is the only one who has turned up:

Look at this! Main Meeting of the Assembly due to start at dawn and not a soul here on the Pnyx. They're all down in the Marketplace gossiping, or dodging the red rope [a painted rope dragged by the squad of Scythian archers, who kept order on Assembly days and on other occasions]. Even the *prytaneis* haven't arrived. They'll arrive late, then they'll come pouring in and push and shove each other to get on the front row. . . . But me, I'm always first to get here to the Assembly. I sit myself down, and then when I see I'm still on my own I sigh and I yawn, then I have a stretch and a fart, and then I don't know what to do; so I scribble a bit, pull a few hairs out, tot up my debts, but my mind is on the fields out there, and I'm longing for peace. I hate the city and I'm longing for my village.

(Aristophanes, *Acharnians* 19–33)

To be amusing this had to be pretty close to reality! But why was Dikaiopolis always there first? The point is that he is a farmer who has been compelled to move into the city behind the Long Walls because of the annual Spartan invasion of Attica and the destruction of farms and crops; and this has been going on now for five years. He is used to getting up early, and he is scornful of those who don't.

In the *Wasps*, produced in 422, Aristophanes gives a picture of the life of a dikast in the courts. Philokleon ('Kleon-lover'; Kleon was a prominent anti-aristocratic politician) is stressing how powerful the dikasts are:

Is there anything more fortunate or more blessed than a dikast? Is there anybody more pampered or more powerful, even when he is an old man? I've just crept out of bed in the morning, and there are these big, six-foot tall men waiting for me at the court entrance, and as I approach one of them slips his hand, the very hand that has stolen from public funds, delicately into mine. They bow and scrape, with a torrent of wheedling words. . . . When I've listened to their pleas I go inside . . . and there's no limit to the flattery you hear as a dikast! Some weep about their poverty, and really pile on the agony, until they make out they're as poor as I am! . . . They even bring in their children, little boys and girls, by the hand . . . and then the father, trembling, begs me as if I were a god to think of his little children and to acquit him and pass his accounts.

(Aristophanes, *Wasps* 550–71)

The 'big six-footers' were men who had held office the previous year and whose *euthynai* were being questioned. The point of being there early if you were to appear in court was that the dikasts were chosen on a 'first come, first served' basis, and if you wanted to bribe or cajole a dikast it made sense to catch those who arrived early and were therefore likely to be chosen for duty in the court.

A little later Philokleon mentions the pay (three obols a day by this time), which was obviously important if you were as poor as he was:

But the sweetest pleasure of all, which I forgot to mention, is when I go home with my pay. As soon as I arrive everybody welcomes me – because of the money. First my daughter washes me and anoints my feet and bends over and kisses me and calls me 'Daddy', and gets my three obols out of me, and

my old woman pets me and fetches me a barley scone and sits
beside me and says, 'Eat this, get your teeth into it'.

(Aristophanes, Wasps 605–12)

Earlier in the play the same point is made more poignantly,
when a little boy has told his father (one of the chorus of old
men, the waspish dikasts of the title of the play) that he wants
some dried figs and not a toy, but gets neither:

Boy Well then, father, if the arkhon is not holding a court today,
   how shall we buy any lunch? Do you have some good plan
   for us . . .?

Chorus Oh dear, oh dear! No, I don't have any idea where our
   next meal is coming from.

(Aristophanes, Wasps 303–11)

'The Old Oligarch'

The short text usually called 'The Old Oligarch' is a fascinating
critique of Athenian democracy, probably written in the 420s.
The title given in the manuscripts is 'The Constitution of
Athens', and the author was in the hellenistic period thought
to be Xenophon (*c.* 428–354), a historian, apparently quite
wealthy, and a friend of Socrates. He left Athens in 401 and
subsequently lived in Sparta and Corinth, probably because he
did not like the restored democracy which emerged after the
Peloponnesian War. Though from his background it does not
seem unreasonable to attribute the work to him, the style of
'The Old Oligarch' is quite definitely not Xenophon's. Who
actually did write it we do not know. But he was certainly no
enthusiast for democracy. His vocabulary makes his attitude
clear; the aristocracy (our own word, of course, comes from
Greek, meaning 'rule of the best', though this actual word is not
used in 'The Old Oligarch') are referred to by several different
words meaning 'the best', 'the finest people', 'the respectable
people', whilst the rest are 'the poor' (objective at least, though
not all supporters of the democracy were poor), 'the worse
element', 'the worthless people', 'the mob', or even once 'the
madmen'. And yet he makes the point, not just once but
repeatedly, that given that Athens *is* a democracy, then it is quite
well run and is at least consistent in its aims of favouring the

demos. His opening paragraph makes the point (and also illustrates the slightly rambling style):

> As far as the Athenian constitution is concerned, I object to their choice of this form of constitution for this reason, that in choosing this constitution they also choose to favour the mob rather than the respectable people; so that is the reason I object to it. But since this is what they have decided to do, I shall show that, even when the other Greeks think they are organising everything the wrong way, they are in fact using the best means of preserving their constitution.
>
> ('The Old Oligarch' i.1)

He then admits that democracy *is* the appropriate form of government for Athens!

> First of all I will say this, that it is right that in Athens the poor and the common people think they should have more power than the noble and rich, and for this reason, that it is the common people who provide rowers for the ships and it is on them that the power of the city is based.
>
> (i.2)

and the Assembly and the Council *should* logically therefore be open to all citizens:

> Some people may think that they ought not to allow everybody to speak in the Assembly and to serve on the Council, but only the most able and the best people. But here too they are arranging things in their own best interests in allowing even the worst elements to speak. For if the respectable people spoke and served on the Council, this would be fine for those like them, but not fine at all for the common people.
>
> (i.6)

He has some odd comments on culture and the *leitourgiai*:

> The common people have no time for those who practise physical exercise and cultural pursuits. They disapprove of all this because they know that they cannot cope with it. On the other hand, they realise that, where it is a matter of providing choral and dramatic festivals or putting on athletic contests or of equipping a trireme, it is the rich who put up the money

while the common people enjoy their festivals and contests and are provided with their triremes.

(i.13)

'On the other hand' attempts to conceal his quite illogical argument – unless, of course, he thought Aeschylos, Sophocles and Euripides were *not* cultural pursuits! But he summarises very neatly the *leitourgiai* system.

The amount of business the Assembly, the Council, the law-courts and the numerous committees had to deal with was huge, and progress could be slow:

I also know that some people criticise the Athenians because sometimes it is impossible to get business settled by the Council or the Assembly even if you have been waiting for a year. This does happen in Athens for no other reason than that, because of the sheer volume of business, those respons-ible for getting things done cannot deal with everybody's request. And how could they, when they are committed to celebrating more festivals than any other city in Greece, and during these festivals it is impossible to transact any public business? And also they have to judge more public and private lawsuits and examine more officials [the *euthynai* process] than in the rest of Greece put together. And on top of that the Council has to take frequent decisions about war, finance, legislation, and about the constant stream of business from Athens and from the allies, and to receive tribute and to administer the dockyards and the temples. So then it is hardly surprising if under such a weight of public affairs it is impossible to settle everybody's business.

(iii.1–2)

A very eloquent summary of the work of the Assembly, the Council and its committees. A little later the author adds yet more detail:

And an enquiry also has to be held if someone fails to equip his trireme, or if someone builds on public land. In addition to this, every year it has to be decided who will finance the chorus at the Dionysia, the Thargelia, the Panathenaia, the Promethia and the Hephaistia. And each year four hundred trierarchs are chosen, and each year an enquiry must be held for those who want it [presumably for an *antidosis*, an

74

exchange of property]. In addition to this magistrates have to be scrutinised [the *dokimasia* process] and enquiries held [if the *euthynai* are not satisfactory].

Despite the complaining tone which pervades much of the work (it is only fourteen pages long in a modern text) and the frequent airing of aristocratic prejudices, we do get a quite detailed picture of the working of the Athenian democracy (and also of the Athenian imperial system, though we have not looked at those sections). The work is equally important for the insight it gives into some aspects of the opposition there was to the democracy; 'The Old Oligarch' was not on his own in his views, and there were many from the old aristocratic families (and also from other sectional groups) who did not even share his admission that it did work reasonably well and did have some justice in it. In 411 some of the opponents of democracy did overthrow the democratic system and set up an oligarchy of 400, but it made a worse mess than the democracy had ever done and used terror tactics into the bargain, so that after a short period of more moderate rule by 5,000 of the more wealthy citizens the full democracy was restored in 410. But Athens still lost the Peloponnesian War in 404; the democracy had no monopoly of sensible decisions, and did indeed make some appalling ones.

6

An overview

In 404 Athens suffered defeat by Sparta and the Peloponnesian League. The democracy in Athens was replaced by a committee of thirty ('The Thirty Tyrants') appointed by the Spartans and Athens became a member of the Peloponnesian League. It seemed that that was the end of the Athenian democracy. But the Thirty Tyrants maliciously set about settling personal scores and grabbing what they could, and in 403 a rebellion broke out, fostered by exiled democrats who had fled to neighbouring Boeotia. The democrats soon occupied Peiraieus and then defeated the forces of the Thirty Tyrants which were sent to quell them. The Spartans had the sense to realise that there was little to be gained from supporting the corrupt and vicious regime of the Thirty, and allowed the democracy to be restored. One of its early measures (in 403–2) was the introduction of a payment of one obol – a sixth of a drachma, not a lot – for each attendance at the Assembly (or to be precise for the first 6,000 to turn up at each meeting of the Assembly), presumably to encourage attendance. But this seems to have been ineffective (if you were not very interested in going, you would not go for an obol!) and very quickly it was increased to three obols, the same rate as for dikasts attending the courts. This did the trick, and in 392 Aristophanes in the *Ekklesiazousai* (lines 300–3), made fun of the crush there now was to get into the meetings of the Assembly. But all this is an interesting commentary on the apathy that had set in after the defeat of 404. Nevertheless, the democracy continued until 322/1, when Antipater, Alexander's successor in Macedonia, quelled a rebellion in Athens and insisted on a change to the constitution which set a property qualification on full Athenian citizenship, reducing those eligible to vote in the Assembly by about a half. The old democracy was in effect dead.

If we are to assess the Athenian democracy, for our purposes from its performance in the fifth century BC, what criteria should we use? Perhaps the following, though far from exhaustive, are useful:

1 How far did the people of Athens feel involved in government?
2 How far did the democracy create a sense of unified purpose for Athenians?
3 Was the democracy efficient, e.g. in use of resources, in getting things done?

Though these areas do overlap, we can to some extent isolate them for assessment purposes.

A sense of involvement

It is, of course, a common criticism of Athenian democracy that metics, women and slaves were excluded from citizenship rights. In terms of numbers, it seems that during the fifth century the number of adult male citizens varied between 30,000 and 50,000 out of a total population of around 250,000 to 300,000. There were perhaps 80,000 slaves (some estimates are over 100,000), and about 25,000 metics (men, women and their families). Adult male citizens were probably no more than 30 per cent of the total adult population. In assessing Athenian democracy we must beware of imposing current views on ancient Greek society. Slavery as an institution was very rarely questioned in the ancient world, even by Christians; in ancient Greece it was simply accepted as part of the fabric of existence. Plato, for instance, in the *Republic* simply assumes there will be slaves in his ideal state, and no Greek of the time would have thought otherwise. So the thought of slaves having any kind of citizen rights just did not occur to Greeks.

The case of women is more complex. In the *Republic* Plato suggests (section 451 ff.) that in his ideal state women will be

77

equal in status to men – though we must remember that Plato's ideal state is not a democracy. Aristophanes also has some interesting views. In the *Ekklesiazousai* (The Assemblywomen), produced as we have seen probably in 392, he bases the whole play on the notion of a takeover of the Assembly by women, and interestingly some ideas in the play closely resemble Plato's proposals in the *Republic* (written about 380). The idea that women might have some political power was clearly conceivable. One might also add that the portrayal of women by the tragedians shows that women were certainly not seen as mere ciphers. The fact remains, however, that women did not have any political rights in the Athenian democracy, and scarcely any legal rights either; in law they were always regarded as being under the guardianship of a male member of the family. An Athenian might well have argued that the concept of individuals exercising citizenship was of far less consequence than the notion that a *family* through its male citizen members was able to express its views.

The metics, people of foreign origin resident in Athens, got a raw deal. Not only did they have no political rights, they also had to contribute to the state in the form of a metic tax (*metoikion*) of twelve drachmas per year for men and six drachmas for women (a drachma, it is worth remembering, was a day's wage for a skilled labourer), and they were eligible for military service and for the liturgy of *choregia*. Metics had to have an Athenian citizen as a sponsor (*prostates*), and they had to register in the deme in which they lived. They could not own property in Attica, and they could not marry an Athenian citizen. In fact, most metics were engaged in manufacturing industries or in trade (or both), and they do seem to have made a good living in what was after all the most prosperous state in the Greek world. They were undoubtedly put upon, but they must have found life in Athens economically worthwhile.

For the 30,000–50,000 adult male citizens, however, involvement in government was there for the taking within the elaborate democratic system we have been analysing. The *dikasteria*, despite their large membership, were always fully manned, and there was even competition to be on the jury panels. The *Boule* was always up to its full quota of 500 members. The daily pay for dikasts and for members of the *Boule* was doubtless an incentive for many, but the purpose of the pay was indeed to ensure that even the poorest citizens could carry out such duties and play a full part in the democracy, and it seems to have achieved that purpose admirably.

The citizens of Athens, then, did feel involved in government. In response to the exclusion from political life of slaves, women and metics, a typical male adult citizen would probably have said that his slaves were, to put it bluntly, politically irrelevant, his family, including the female members, were well represented in that he and his immediate male adult relatives could attend the Assembly and could from time to time hold some office, and the metics could leave if they didn't like it.

A sense of unified purpose

The Athenian Assembly definitely seems to have achieved a sense of unified purpose. The leading politicians, in particular Themistocles, Kimon and Pericles, put before the Assembly a policy of expansion and of imperial control over the islands and coasts of the Aegean. And in the democracy the citizen body not only voted for such heady policies but were also the people who carried them out as crews on the triremes. Even after Pericles' death and through the long years of the Peloponnesian War the Assembly maintained a surprising confidence in its ability to win the war, even in the later years when any objective analysis must have revealed problems of Athenian resources and an increasing control of the seas by the Spartan naval forces which, barring some quite remarkable reversal of fortune, were leading inexorably towards a crushing defeat. The Assembly always felt that it was definitely in charge – and so it was. When it made mistakes there was no-one else to blame, though it was never slow to blame those who did not carry out its policies as effectively as it thought they should. In 411, after the disaster of the Sicilian Expedition, with a Spartan force in permanent occupation of Dekeleia, and with many of their allies in revolt, the Four Hundred oligarchs took over the government of Athens, thinking that a small group of 'better' people could do a better job than the democracy. In fact the Four Hundred quickly split into factions and were totally ineffective; they had no common purpose amongst themselves, and they could not come up with policies that were remotely acceptable beyond their small factions. In 410 the full democracy was restored.

True, this did not result in victory in the Peloponnesian War, but at least a common resolve was revived. The very fact that for a policy decision to be implemented a majority of the Assembly had to vote for it meant that, by definition, most of those who were in the Assembly to hear the arguments and to vote were responsible, and *directly* responsible, for what was done. Even if the sense of purpose was not always common to all, it was common to a majority.

Efficiency

'The Old Oligarch', as we saw earlier, does say that 'sometimes it is impossible to get business settled by the Council or the Assembly even if you have been waiting for a year' (iii.1). But even he, critic of the system as he was, only says 'sometimes'! Democratic systems can be slow, simply because decisions have to be made by the statutory bodies and through agreed procedures, and the Athenian democracy was certainly no exception.

It is useful to remind ourselves of the scale of the state of Athens. The Athenian democracy controlled not only the governmental institutions, the public finance, the state festivals and the legal system for the whole population of Attica, but also organised the tribute system for the Delian League and operated a fleet of around 300 triremes. We know that the Athenian internal annual budget (that is, excluding the tribute from the Delian League) was about 400 talents just before the outbreak of the Peloponnesian War, and the Delian League tribute totalled 600 talents at that time, though this rose to 1,400 talents in 425. It is always difficult to give any meaningful comparisons in economic matters between the ancient world and today, but, to use a comparison we used earlier, and totalling the internal and Delian League incomes, this means that the annual disposable income of Athens was enough to pay 20,000 labourers in 431, and 36,000 labourers in 425. As a state, Athens was bigger than the modern state of Iceland, and probably close to the size of Luxemburg, and of course had the additional responsibility of the Delian League.

We can perhaps highlight just a few areas where we have evidence for efficiency in at least some sense of the word. The allies would pretty certainly have agreed, doubtless grudgingly after peace was made with Persia in 449, that the Athenian fleet was an efficient military force, and the members of the Peloponnesian League in 431 would have gone along with that. In public art and culture, if one can apply the concept of efficiency here, there is little doubt that the spending of public money resulted in some quite outstanding feats of architecture and drama (and probably of music, which is now lost), and many have indeed argued that such artistic quality could not have arisen without the democracy (though that is a rather different and perhaps less tangible argument). And, given that the Athenian democracy required the direct involvement of large numbers of citizens, including the very poorest, both in politics and in the operation of the legal system, it might be argued that the modest outlay of their basic daily expenses when citizens were engaged on state business was a very efficient way of running a democracy and at the same time providing a form of employment and a modicum of state support for large numbers of poor citizens.

This is admittedly a favourable assessment, and the people of Mytilene, and certainly those of Melos, would have had something different to say. But no political system can guarantee that people will always act sensibly, humanely, or even in their own corporate interests. At least in the Athenian democracy more people were given a chance to try than in most other political systems.

Today there is a tendency to look back at Athenian democracy as the fountainhead of all modern democracies. But such ideas need to be evaluated with caution. As far as the ancient world was concerned Athenian democracy was seen by later historians as an interesting experiment, but not particularly favoured by many. Neither Plato nor Aristotle, both of whom lived in the Athenian democracy, saw it as the best form of government; and, as one might expect, democracy was not at all popular with hellenistic monarchs or Roman senators, and certainly not with Roman emperors. In the medieval world the very idea of democracy was hardly mentioned, except as an oddity of classical Athens. Modern democracies did not develop out of admiration for Athenian democracy but had their own long, tortuous and difficult histories. So there is no continuity in the development of a democratic ideal, and we have to remember that this ideal is not by any means shared by everybody today.

Whether democracy is in fact a good thing is ultimately a matter of value judgement, of the value we put on individual citizens and on their right to be involved in the organisation and decision-making of the society in which they live. In 508/7 Kleisthenes was persuaded (willingly or not) that these were indeed the values which the Athenian constitution should reflect, and as we have seen the Athenian democracy worked for nearly two centuries. But democracy is not some kind of natural progression which the Athenians happen to have stumbled on first. Its values have to be reasserted in every generation.

Appendix 1
Kleisthenic tribes, *trittyes*, demes and Council members

The information in the following table is based on Traill, J.S. (1975) *The Political Organisation of Attica* (Hesperia Supplement XIV), Princeton, for the American School of Classical Studies at Athens.

For each tribe all demes are shown, divided into City, Coast and Inland *trittyes*. The location of each *trittys* can be found on Map 3.

Against each deme is recorded the number of members of the Council of 500 allocated to the deme, and the total of members for each *trittys* is given at the foot of each *trittys* column. Where the number of members from a deme is given as, for example, 3/4, this indicates that the number varied in alternate years (in the case of III Pandionis in a three year cycle); in effect the allocation of a member was shared with another deme within the tribe (not necessarily within the same *trittys*). The total of members of the Council for each tribe is, of course, fifty.

After the name of each tribe the number in square brackets indicates the total number of demes in the tribe. Totals of demes in each *trittys* are given in square brackets at the foot of each *trittys* column.

City		Coast		Inland	
I Erechtheis [14]					
Upper Agryle	2	Anagyrous	6	Kephisia	6
Lower Agryle	3	Kedoi	2	Upper Pergase	2
Euonymon	10	Upper Lamptrai	5	Lower Pergase	2
Themakos	1	Coastal Lamptrai	9	Phegous	1
[4]		Pambotadai	0/1	Sybridai	0/1
		[5]		[5]	
	16		22/23		11/12
II Aigeis [21]					
Upper Ankyle	1	Araphen	2	Erchia	6/7
Lower Ankyle	1	Halai Araphenides	5	Gargettos	4
Bate	1/2			Ikarion	4/5
Diomeia	1	Otryne	1	Ionidai	1/2
Erikeia	1	Phegaia	3/4	Kydantidai	1/2
Hestiaia	1	Philaidai	3	Myrrhinoutta	1
Kollytos	3	[5]		Plotheia	1
Kolonos	2			Teithras	4
[8]				[8]	
	11/12		14/15		24/25
III Pandionis [11]					
Kydathenaion	11/12	Angele	2/3	Konthyle	1
[1]		Myrrhinous	6	Kytheros	1/2
		Prasiai	3	Oa	4
		Probalinthos	5	Upper Paiania	1
		Steiria	3	Lower Paiania	11
		[5]		[5]	
	11/12		19/20		18/19
IV Leontis [20]					
Halimous	3	Deiradiotai	2	Aithalidai	2
Kettos	3	Potamos Deiradiotes	2	Cholleidai	2
Leukonion	3			Eupyridai	2
Oion Kerameikon	1	Upper Potamos	2	Hekale	1
Skambonidai	3	Lower Potamos	1	Hybadai	2
[5]		Phrearrhioi	9	Kolonai	2
		Sounion	4	Kropidai	1
		[6]		Paionidai	3
				Pelekes	2
				[9]	
	13		20		17
V Akamantis [13]					
Cholargos	4	Kephale	9	Eitea	2
Eiresidai	1	Poros	3	Hagnous	5
Hermos	2	Thorikos	5	Kikynna	2
Iphistiadai	1	[3]		Prospalta	5
Kerameis	6			Sphettos	5
[5]				[5]	
	14		17		19

84

City		Coast		Inland	
VI Oineis [13]					
Boutadai	1	Kothokidai	1/2	Acharnai	22
Epikephisia	1/2	Oe	6/7	[1]	
Hippotomadai	1	Phyle	2		
Lakiadai	2	Thria	7		
Lousia	1	[4]			
Perithoidai	3				
Ptelea	1				
Tyrmeidai	0/1				
[8]					
	11		17		22
VII Kekropis [11]					
Daidalidai	1	Aixone	9?	Athmonon	5?
Melite	7	Halai Aixonides	6	Epieikidai	1
Xypete	7	[2]		Phlya	7
[3]				Pithos	3
				Sypalettos	2
				Trinemeia	2?
				[6]	
	15		15?		20?
VIII Hippothontis [17]					
Hamaxanteia	1	Acherdous	1	Anakaia	3
Keiriadai	2	Auridai	1	Dekeleia	4
Koile	3	Azenia	2	Eroiadai	1
Korydallos	2?	Elaious	1	Oion Dekeleikon	3
Peiraieus	9	Eleusis	11	[4]	
Thumaitadai	2	Kopros	2		
[6]		Oinoe	2		
		[7]			
	19?		20		11
IX Aiantis [6]					
Phaleron	9	Marathon	10	Aphidna	16
[1]		Oinoe	4	[1]	
		Rhamnous	8		
		Trikorynthos	3		
		[4]			
	9		25		16
X Antiochis [13]					
Alopeke	10	Aigilia	6	Eitea	1/2
[1]		Amphitrope	2	Eroiadai	1
		Anaphlystos	10	Kolonai	2
		Atene	3	Krioa	1
		Besa	2	Pallene	6/7
		Thorai	4	Semachidai	1
		[6]		[6]	
	10		27		13

Appendix 2
Ostracisms

We do not possess a complete list of ostracisms. The following list of people who were ostracised is based on literary and epigraphical sources, though dates are in several cases unsure.

487 HIPPARCHOS, who had been arkhon in 496/5. His mother was probably the daughter of Hippias, the tyrant of Athens 527–510, and this connection was most probably at least one reason for his ostracism.

486 MEGACLES, head of the Alkmeonid family at the time, nephew and son-in-law of Kleisthenes and uncle of Pericles. He won the four-horse chariot race at the Pythian Games at Delphi this same year and his victory is celebrated in Pindar's seventh Pythian Ode, in which there is a veiled reference to the fact that Megacles has just been exiled from Athens. We know nothing of his political activities.

485 KALLIXENOS (perhaps), another member of the Alkmeonid family, unknown from literary sources but very well represented in the finds of ostraca from the *agora* in Athens; one calls him 'traitor'. Since the *Athenaion Politeia* (22.6) implies there was also an ostracism in 485 of 'a friend of the tyrants', Kallixenos seems a likely candidate.

484 XANTHIPPOS, father of Pericles, married to Agariste, niece of Kleisthenes, and doubtless exiled for his support of the Alkmeonids even though he was not himself from the family.

All four of the above were apparently exiled because of connections with the Peisistratids (presumably with Hippias), but one suspects the Alkmeonids were again showing signs of wanting to take over everything they could.

482 ARISTEIDES, one of the generals at Marathon, arkhon in 489/8, opposed Themistocles' plans for expanding the navy, and this was almost certainly the reason for his exile.

471 THEMISTOCLES, arkhon 493/2, a general at Marathon, developed Athenian navy and was mainly responsible for the victory at Salamis in 480. After that he lost ground to Kimon and the aristocrats. After his ostracism in 471 he lived for a time in Argos. He was then accused by the Athenians of collaborating with the Persians and sentenced to death. He fled to Asia Minor (c.468) and became governor of a Persian province there. He died there c.462.

461 KIMON, son of Miltiades of Marathon fame, rose to prominence after 479. General of his tribe many times from 478, and very active in most Athenian naval campaigns. Lost the support of the Assembly because of his friendship with Sparta, and as a result of the failure of the expedition to help Sparta to subdue a slave revolt in 462. Returned to Athens probably in the late 450s. Died in an expedition to Cyprus c.450.

443 THUCYDIDES, son of Melesias, related by marriage to Kimon. Led the aristocratic faction after Kimon's death and opposed Pericles, especially in his policy of using money from the allies to carry out the extensive building programme on the Acropolis and elsewhere. Pericles called for an ostracism, and successfully got rid of Thucydides.

417 HYPERBOLOS, a demagogue who gained much influence with the Assembly after Cleon's death in 421. In 417 an ostracism took place in which Hyperbolos apparently hoped to remove Nikias or Alcibiades, but his opponents joined forces against him and he was exiled. Hyperbolos went to Samos where he was murdered by revolutionary oligarchs. The ostracism was seen as something of a farce, and it was not used again thereafter.

Bibliography

What follows is far from being a full bibliography of Athenian democracy, which would be an almost impossible task even if we restricted ourselves to the period ending with the defeat of Athens in 404. The aim of this short bibliography is to give some account of the main ancient sources for our knowledge of the development of Athenian democracy and its operation to the end of the Peloponnesian War, together with a selection of some of the modern works on the subject which have been chosen for their ready availability or for their particular importance for some aspect of the subject.

Ancient sources

In chronological order the main literary sources are the following:

SOLON: the fragments of Solon's poetry are most readily available in West, M.L. (1994) *Greek Lyric Poetry* (World's Classics Series), Oxford: Oxford University Press. The Greek text is in West, M.L. (1989–92) *Iambi et Elegi Graeci* (2nd edn.), Oxford: Oxford University Press.

HERODOTUS: most easily available in Aubrey de Selincourt (trans.) (1954) *Herodotus: The Histories*, Harmondsworth: Penguin Classics. The Greek text is in two volumes in the

Oxford Classical Texts (OCT) series (1927). Herodotus deals with the Persian Wars and the background to them. He lived about 490–425. He came from Halikarnassos in Ionia, but he seems to have lived in Athens in the 440s and to have known Pericles. He is an important source for the events of the sixth century, and he strongly supports the Alkmeonid family, perhaps because his sources in Athens were connected with the family. However, he gives us surprisingly little information on the working of the democracy.

THUCYDIDES: available in Rex Warner (trans.) (1954) *The Peloponnesian War*, Harmondsworth: Penguin Classics. The Greek text is in two volumes in the OCT series (1942). Thucydides was an Athenian, born around 460. He was a general in 424, but exiled after his failure to defend Amphipolis against the Spartans that year. He was, of course, fully aware of how the democracy worked, though he rarely gives any details of procedures.

ARISTOPHANES: in three volumes in the Penguin Classics series: David Barrett (trans.) (1964) *The Frogs and Other Plays*; Sommerstein, A.H. (trans.) (1973) *Lysistrata/The Acharnians/The Clouds*; David Barrett and Sommerstein, A.H. (trans.) (1978) *The Knights/Peace/The Assemblywomen/Wealth*. The Greek text is in two volumes in the OCT series (1906 and 1907). Aristophanes' extant plays cover the period 425 to 382. Most of the plays contain material which gives us insights into the way the democracy worked.

'THE OLD OLIGARCH': the most accessible translation is Hughes, K.R., Thorpe, M. and Thorpe, M.A. (rev. edn 1986) *The Old Oligarch* (LACTOR 2), London: London Association of Classical Teachers. The Greek text is in *Xenophontis V: Opuscula* (1920) in the OCT series. The work is a pamphlet written probably in the 420s as a critique of Athenian democracy. The author is unknown, but he is clearly not much in sympathy with the system.

ARISTOTLE: the work entitled *Athenaion Politeia* ('The Athenian Constitution') is not actually by Aristotle, but probably by one of his pupils. There is a translation with introduction and notes in the Penguin Classics series by Rhodes, P.J. (1984). The Greek text is in the OCT series under the title *Aristotelis Atheniensium*

Respublica (1920). The work was written between 332 and 322 and consists of two parts, the first (about two-thirds of the book) on the history of the system, and the second on the way the constitution worked in the author's own times. It is an invaluable source of information on every aspect of the Athenian democracy, though it is not without errors, and it has to be used with caution.

Aristotle's *Politics* is essentially a treatise on political theory, but it does contain material specifically on the Athenian constitution and how it worked. It is available in the Penguin Classics series as Aristotle, *The Politics*, trans. Sinclair, T.A. and revised by Saunders, T.J. (1981). The index gives all important references to Athenian democracy. There is a Greek text under the title *Aristotelis Politica* (1957) in the OCT series.

PLUTARCH: a Greek biographer, historian and moral philosopher who lived *c.* AD 46–120. Fifty of his biographies survive, mostly written in pairs with one Greek and one Roman statesman who are then compared by Plutarch. He was, of course, writing long after the sixth and fifth centuries BC and his moralising rather overshadows historical accuracy; he himself admitted that he did not let strict chronology ruin a good story! Nevertheless, he used many sources now lost to us and his *Lives* are full of intriguing if sometimes dubious detail. The *Lives* most relevant for a study of Athenian democracy are those of Solon, Themistocles, Aristides, Kimon and Pericles; all these are to be found in Plutarch, *The Rise and Fall of Athens: Nine Greek Lives*, trans. Scott-Kilvert, I. (1960) in the Penguin Classics series. There is a Greek text with English translation in the Loeb series under the title *Plutarch: The Parallel Lives*, trans. Perrin, B. (Solon in vol. 1, Themistocles, Aristides and Kimon in vol. 2, and Pericles in vol. 3).

Inscriptions from Athens and Attica have provided much evidence for the procedures of the democracy, in the form of decrees of the Assembly, lists of buildings accounts, temple dedications, and numerous decrees of the deme councils. Examples can be found in MEIGGS, R. and LEWIS, D. (1969) *Greek Historical Inscriptions to the End of the Fifth Century*, Oxford: Oxford University Press, though one needs a good grasp of Greek since the inscriptions are not translated. A selection of inscriptions, in English translation this time, is also to be found in

HORNBLOWER, S. and GREENSTOCK, M.C. (3rd edn 1984) *The Athenian Empire* (LACTOR 1), London: London Association of Classical Teachers, and several are in fact translations of inscriptions which are in Meiggs and Lewis, though the range is, as the title indicates, restricted to those relevant to the Athenian Empire.

A most useful book containing virtually all relevant primary sources, in English translation, for the period down to 500 BC is STANTON, G.R. (1990) *Athenian Politics c.800–500: A Sourcebook*, London: Routledge. There are also very full commentaries on each source.

Modern sources

CLAYTON, R.W. (ed.) (1973) *Athenian Politics: Democracy in Athens from Pericles to Cleophon* (LACTOR 5), London: London Association of Classical Teachers, is a useful collection of translated primary source materials with a brief introduction to each section and notes on each translated source.

FORREST, W.G. (1966) *The Emergence of Greek Democracy*, London: Weidenfeld and Nicolson, has a very readable narrative account of how the concept and practice of democracy developed in Athens from 800 to 400 BC.

HANSEN, M.H. (1991) *The Athenian Democracy in the Age of Demosthenes*, Oxford: Blackwell, must be mentioned, despite its concentration on the later stages of the democracy. This is a very detailed account of the Athenian democracy, with much information from the fifth century. Its bibliography is massive, with over 700 works listed (68 by Hansen himself).

HIGNET, C. (1951) *A History of the Athenian Constitution to the End of the Fifth Century* BC, Oxford: Oxford University Press, has in many details been superseded by more recent work, but it remains a classic of its time and presents a very clear chronological account of how the Athenian democracy developed.

JONES, A.H.M. (1978) *Athenian Democracy*, Oxford: Blackwell, is a collection of five separate papers on aspects of Athenian democracy in the fifth and fourth centuries. Chapters II and IV are specifically on the fourth century, but the other three chapters have much useful detail on the working of the democracy in the fifth century as well as the fourth.

JONES, P.V. (ed.) (1984) *The World of Athens*, Cambridge: Cambridge University Press, is a useful general work, with a very good summary of Athenian democracy in Section 5.

STOCKTON, D. (1990) *The Classical Athenian Democracy*, Oxford: Oxford University Press, is the most accessible survey of Athenian democracy currently available. This book concentrates on the fifth century.

TRAILL, J.S. (1975) *The Political Organisation of Attica* (Hesperia Supplement XIV), Princeton, for the American School of Classical Studies at Athens, is a meticulous study of the organisation of the Kleisthenic tribes into demes and *trittyes*, together with the allocation of Council members from each deme and *trittys*. For anyone who really wants to know the geographical detail of how the tribal system operated this work is essential.

WHITEHEAD, D. (1986) *The Demes of Attica 508/7 – c. 250* BC, Princeton: Princeton University Press, is a very detailed study of the local government system in Attica, and is the only book currently available which deals comprehensively with the way demes operated.